JANE ASHER'S
· CHILDREN'S ·
PARTIES

JANE ASHER'S
· CHILDREN'S ·
PARTIES

Pelham Books
LONDON

This book is dedicated to my Mother in appreciation of all the parties she gave for us.

The author and publishers are grateful to the following for permission to reproduce the copyright material: Licensing Corporation of America and D. Dekker Ltd manufacturers of the official Batman and Superman costumes; Postman Pat © Woodland Animations Ltd 1988; He-Man © Mattel Inc (1988). All Rights Reserved; She-Ra © Mattel Inc (1988). All Rights Reserved; Spider-Man © 1988 Marvel Entertainments Group Inc; Thomas the Tank Engine © William Heinemann Ltd 1983 and © Britt Allcroft (Thomas) Ltd 1983; My Little Pony and Transformer cakes Hasbro Industries (UK) Ltd.

All the photographs in this book were taken by James Merrell with the exception of the following: pages 26, 33 (top), 43, 49 which first appeared in *Family Circle*; page 49 (top right) which is by Bryan Wharton.
Costume diagrams by Jill Shipley
Cake diagrams by PanTek

PELHAM BOOKS

Published by the Penguin Group
27 Wrights Lane, London W8 5TZ, England
Viking Penguin Inc., 40 West 23rd Street, New York,
New York 10010, USA ·
Penguin Books Australia Ltd, Ringwood, Victoria, Australia
Penguin Books Canada Ltd, 2801 John Street, Markham, Ontario,
Canada L3R 1B4
Penguin Books (NZ) Ltd, 182–190 Wairau Road, Auckland 10,
New Zealand

Penguin Books Ltd, Registered Offices: Harmondsworth, Middlesex,
England

First published 1988

Copyright © Myriad Productions 1988

Typeset in Horley by Goodfellow & Egan, Cambridge
Printed and bound by Butler & Tanner, Frome, Somerset

ISBN 0 7207 1848 1

A CIP catalogue record for this book is available from the
British Library

CONTENTS

Little Miss Muffet and Mary Mary at the Nursery Rhyme Party (page 32).

ACKNOWLEDGEMENTS

I couldn't have produced this book without the help of a wonderful team. Many thanks once again to Jill Thraves who, just as she did for my Fancy Dress book, translated my costume ideas into easily-made reality, to Winkle Haworth for helping to cook mounds of party food, to Penny Pearson who helped me present it for the photographs (I've never *seen* such finely chopped parsley), to Jenny Alston for translating my cookery ideas into proper recipes, to Janice Springall for making several of the cakes for me (do try and look in at her marvellous shop Imaginative Icing in Scarborough), to Karina Garrick for rushing around London to find colourful paper plates, pretty dresses, streamers, pirate hats and a hundred and one other things, to 'Uncle' Jim for not only being photographed as our entertainer, but keeping many children very happy during the session (to book him yourself see page 126), to Mrs B. Fraser and her staff at the Centre Nursery for letting us take photographs there, to Trish Burgess for keeping the whole book on schedule, to Patricia Walters for managing to squeeze all my photographs and text into one book and for making it look so pretty, to Bo Steer for recruiting many of the children and for ferrying them in shifts to and from the photo sessions, and to James Merrell and his assistant Ian Skelton for photographing everything so patiently.

My good friend Gyles Brandreth generously let me pinch many of the game ideas from his wonderful books – if you become a keen party giver and need more than the 121 games given here I highly recommend two of them: BOOK OF PARTY GAMES and GAMES FOR PARTIES, both published by Knight.

Special thanks to Roger Houghton and John Beaton of Pelham Books for supporting and encouraging me and, as usual, to my family for putting up with the chaos.

Most of all, my love and gratitude to all the children who so sweetly and enthusiastically joined in our 'parties' and were such wonderful models: Samantha Akuwumi; Siobhan Alexander; Polly Allison; Sophie Boston; Lalyn Camara; Emily Cooper; Lydia Davis; Sophie Davis; Perrine D'Avoine; Emily Day; Carleen Freeman; Jesse Garrick; Jenny Grey; B Hankey; Makeda Hagley; Dominic Haworth; Kimberley Haworth; Chelsee Hewitt; Harvey Horner; Holly Horner; Daisy Houghton; Alexander Howard; Chloë Hutchinson; Kolya Hutchinson; Vivene Johnson; Robert Judge; Adam Kaye; Marc Kaye; Nicholas Kelly; Naomi Konu; Simone Konu; Annabel Lawson; Louise Lawson; Verne Lewis; Georgina Lucas; Maya Mailer; James McDermott; Lucy Merrell; Thomas Merrell; Rosalind Moore; Imogen Powley; Jimmy Rahman; Ben Reid; Georgia Robinson; Joanne Sanson; Paul Segal; Natalie Silman; Harry Steer; Jack Steer; Nathan Tetley; Georges Villeneau; Lawrence Vosper; Adanne Wadibia-Anyanwu; Eleanor Walford; Philip Wright.

I am especially grateful to the following shops:

Paperchase
213 Tottenham Court Road
London W1
580-8496

Party tableware, paper accessories, artist's materials. Most of the tablecloths, plates and cups in the photographs came from their marvellous selection.

Oscar's Den
127 Abbey Road
London N1
328-6683

Hire of tables, chairs, high chairs, disco unit. They will also organise entertainers, make up party bags, shop also sells everything for children's parties.

Theatre Zoo
21 Earlham Street
London WC2
836-3150

Costume hire, sells hats, stage make-up, masks, party accessories etc. (including the wonderful bats and skeletons for our Hallowe'en party).

Anthea Moore-Ede
16 Victoria Grove
London W8 5RW
584-8826

Traditional English and French children's clothes. The way you dream your children should look at a party!

Waterford Wedgwood
32/34 Wigmore Street
London W1
486-5181

Wedgwood china – see our elegant twelve-year-old dinner party.

Cotton Candy
Unit 23 Portobello Green Arcade
281 Portobello Road
London W10 5TA
968-9529

Cotton children's wear; lovely comfortable clothes ideal for party-going.

Moss Bros.
21–26 Bedford Street
Covent Garden
London WC2E 9EQ
240-4567

Men's and boys' evening dress hire (see our smart young men on page 70).

Freds
Smith Street
London SW3
730-2754

Older girls'/women's clothes, as worn for our twelve-year-old party. Beautiful dresses and extremely reasonably priced.

INTRODUCTION

There are such high expectations of a children's party – especially from the all-important guest of honour – that instead of the wonderfully happy and exciting day it should be, I often feel it is a huge hurdle that somehow has to be got over. I think I've got better about this in the last few years; after three children and twenty-four birthday parties (what a thought!), not to mention numerous Christmas, Hallowe'en and Easter parties I'm getting the balance about right. If I decide to splash out and get an entertainer to organise the whole party then fine – I won't feel guilty. If, on the other hand, I plan and carry out the whole thing myself because I'm feeling unusually full of energy and optimism then that's fine too; if the food's a disaster and the games met with stony faces I shan't be unduly upset.

But there's no doubt some judicious pre-planning pays off, and the more you can arrange ahead of time the more you will manage to enjoy the birthday itself, and to watch your child at the peak of excitement and joy on such a very special day. I remember being almost sick with excitement as my birthday approached. (If only I still felt that way; there's no doubt the charm of the whole thing loses its edge somewhere around thirty . . .)

I do hope the ideas and recipes in this book will help you to have some happy parties. Most of the food and games are interchangeable; I have divided them into age groups and themes to make it simpler, but do browse through them all before planning your own particular party. You'll also find plenty of alternative recipes at the back of the book – including some sugar-free cake ideas for children who cannot tolerate sugar. Try to pre-plan as much as you can from the first section, but if you can't then don't worry: some of the best parties are the last minute, impromptu ones.

The most important thing of all is that you are relaxed and happy – if you get tense and irritable your child will be miserable. Only too often I find myself shouting at the children and being impatient with them, and on a birthday it just isn't fair. If your grand cake went wrong, you forgot to get balloons or the children have spilt a whole packet of lentils all over the carpet *don't let it upset you*. Laugh it off and have fun – you can clear up the lentils tomorrow . . .

PRE-PLANNING

TIME

Choose the date first of all. If the child you are giving the party for is at school you may have to consider a weekend or holiday – it can be much too tiring to have a party during the week, particularly once homework starts. Be careful of choosing the middle of the holidays as you may find too many friends will be away; a date near to the beginning or just after the end of term is usually more successful.

Children's parties are usually associated with tea time, and certainly the traditional afternoon party is the most common. What time the party starts and finishes depends to a large extent on the age of the child, whether he or she still has an afternoon nap, what time school ends and so on. The amount of excitement and entertainment that young ones can take in one afternoon increases as they get older, and it's always better to have the party too short rather than too long. I tended to be over ambitious when I had our first few celebrations and often found that I and the children were flagging and looking rather jaded long before the appointed end of the festivities. If they start asking for their going home bags when you're just about to bring out the birthday cake you'll know you've overdone it.

But you don't have to stick to tea time: over the last few years I've given many lunchtime parties instead, and they've proved very successful. The children tend to be less tired, to eat and play more enthusiastically and when the guests have gone there is still time for the birthday person to open his or her presents and enjoy the closing stages of 'the great day' without bedtime rushing up too fast. Strangely enough, it's also a much easier meal to prepare; one main savoury dish and a puddingy sort of cake are far simpler than preparing sandwiches, biscuits and little cakes.

PLACE

As for where to give it: as a general rule I would say there's no place like home. It obviously depends very largely on the age group and numbers you are entertaining and the amount of space you have available as to whether this is practicable. You certainly don't want twenty-five eleven-year-olds playing a cross between American football and World War III in a small elegant living room. If you are at all worried about space it's worth checking well ahead of time into the sort of rooms that may be available for hire locally – church and village halls, hotel 'function' rooms, restaurants, even schools are all worth considering. Or perhaps you know a friend who has a large room in her house that you could borrow? I went to a party recently which was given in the garage – it worked extremely well. Once the children are more than two or three you ideally want two rooms that you can use, so the meal and the games can be kept separate. If you do use anywhere other than home, be sure to check it thoroughly first to make sure the children will be warm, comfortable and, above all, safe.

CHOOSING A THEME

There's really no need to base your party on any particular theme, but it can be fun, especially if you choose something the birthday person is particularly keen on at the time. Most of the parties I give are just a fairly jolly sort of mixture, but there's something to be said for taking the trouble to have a 'look' to the settings, food and decorations. Don't ever be too ambitious – there'll be quite enough to do without trying to turn your house into an igloo or an Indian fort; keep it very simple and only ever do as much as will be fun. The children would much rather you were (relatively!) relaxed with things a bit of a shambles than have a designer party with a tired parent.

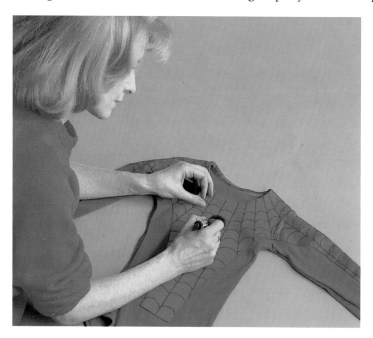

Putting the felt tip web on our Spider-Man costume (see page 123).

NUMBERS

This too varies enormously with age. I think on the whole people tend to invite too many children – I have often made this mistake and at certain ages it can make for a chaotic, divided party. Some say you should invite the same number of children as the age of the birthday person (pretty boring party for a one-year-old) but although this may give a rough guide I don't think it's very accurate. It depends on the character of the child the party is for, the type of friends you are inviting and the place and style of the party, but if in doubt ask less than you think.

INVITATIONS

Make a list of all the children you are inviting to the party together with their addresses and telephone numbers. Even if you are delivering the invitations by hand you may well need to contact some of them nearer the day. Try to send them out in very good time – children's social calendars can get very full, especially once they are at school. Three to four weeks ahead is ideal, but obviously many parties are organised and enjoyed at much shorter notice. Try not to force the child to have anyone to the party that he/she doesn't really want just because not inviting them may be embarrassing for you. Likes and dislikes can be very strong at a young age, and rightly or wrongly a party is not the time to try and change them. If you are not asking the whole class give the invitations to the teacher to slip tactfully into their satchels. (Not that it will do much good; most of the little darlings will no doubt be boasting the next day 'I've been invited to Jennifer's party and you haven't so YOU'RE STUPID!!') It can be very awkward if there is only one person in the class who is not wanted; it would be far

Either buy ready made invitations or make your own with coloured paper, stickers and felt tips.
It's fun to make them to match your 'theme', but keep it simple.

too cruel to allow this. You will need all your skill to get round it; such objections as 'Geoffrey smells and steals my ruler' can be tricky to negotiate.

Don't forget to ask grandparents, aunts and uncles or godparents if they want to come, and younger children may want to invite their schoolteachers.

You can of course just telephone the invitation, but it can be hard to get hold of everyone and once the written invitations are either posted or given to the school you can relax. Do make sure you give all the necessary details as below, and keep a list of whom you have asked pinned up somewhere so you can tick them off as they reply. You'll almost certainly have to ring and check up on one or two who haven't answered near the day. There are many different kinds of invitations that you can buy, but some of them can be very expensive. The pads of tear-off ones tend to be cheaper than the little packs of six or eight or you could make simple ones yourself, with or without the help of the children, depending how patient you are feeling . . .

> To John
>
> Please come to Henry Smith's birthday party
> On December 16th
> From 12.30 - 2.30
>
> At 43, Andrew Street
> W11
> RSVP 937 7255   Fancy Dress

ORGANISING HELP

Very young children of up to three or four will come to parties accompanied by adults who will probably be only too willing to help pour out orange squash, mop up spills and ferry children to the lavatory. Once past that age children are often happy to be left on their own, and you may need to organise extra help. It really isn't much fun running a party single-handed, however small. Relatives and friends are often very happy to help if asked. Ideally you should have at least two helpers, so that two people can organise the games and watch the children while you get the meal ready. At the end of the party someone will need to find the coats, going home bags and balloons while the remaining children are being entertained.

ENTERTAINMENT

There's no doubt, expensive as they are, that professional entertainers are very good value. They usually offer two types of service; either they will run the entire party for you, providing games and music before tea and a show afterwards, or they can be hired just to give a show after the meal. Although it's great fun to do everything yourself, it can be very exhausting, and when we had an entertainer I found I was able to really watch the children enjoying themselves for the first time. Word of mouth is the best way of finding someone, or your child may see one at a friend's party that he/she particularly wants. Or try your local paper or the Yellow Pages. We give a few names at the end of the book. Do book well ahead and if he proves especially successful it's even worth booking straight away for the following year.

Allow plenty of time for the entertainer to get set up – and if possible introduce him to the birthday person.

Don't worry if you can't afford an entertainer; there are plenty of games and ideas in the book to keep a party going, and you will feel very satisfied that you did it all on your own! Alternatively, if you do decide once in a while to hire someone to run it for you, don't feel guilty. After all, *everyone* should enjoy a party.

DECORATIONS

I have never much bothered with extensive decorations for birthday parties – it's quite enough to have to fill everywhere with trees, tinsel and paperchains once a year at

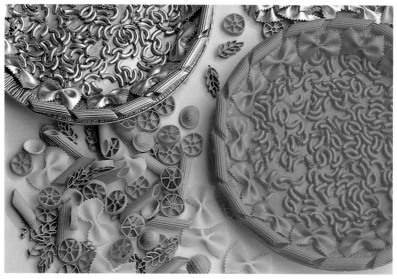

*These pasta plates are easy to make and look wonderful for a colourful party
or at Christmas. Glue pasta shapes on to foil dishes: when dry spray liberally
with gold, silver or coloured paint. Don't put food directly on them – use doyleys
or glass dishes in between.*

Christmas – but a little touch here and there can add enormously to the atmosphere. It's not a time for subtlety; the more gaudy, bright, jolly and big the better. Use lots of balloons and cheap paper streamers, and if you can dig out your Christmas tree lights use them on some shelves or draped at a window; very pub-like but very festive. If you want to echo a particular theme put up some posters or drawings, and attach something suitable to the front door with a big bunch of balloons.

PRESENTS AND PRIZES

If you're going to play any kind of competitive game you'll need prizes. They shouldn't be big or expensive – just little tokens, and if you can avoid sweets, so much the better. They'll no doubt be eating far too many sweet things on the party day as it is. Some of the mail order toy manufacturers will sell big bags of 'lucky dip' toys which work out very cheap, or sometimes local newsagents have good selections of little toys. Keep your eye out in the weeks leading up to the party: you'll need enough for the now obligatory 'going home bags' as well.

FOOD

Young children never seem to eat quite as much as you expect at a party, and I think all parents have found themselves at one time or another left with mountains of sandwiches, cakes and biscuits. Whether it's lunch or tea, keep it very simple – you don't want to be slaving over some complicated dish when there is so much else to do. Listen to your child: if he/she wants macaroni cheese *with* jaffa cakes (a favourite delicacy of my daughter's at one stage) then so be it. Unless it's something unimaginably disgusting, like jelly with gravy, let the birthday person decide the menu. They're more likely to know what their friends like than you are. But try not to serve only sweet foods, children are usually happy to eat more healthy alternatives as long as they are attractively produced.

Food for adults
When the children are young they will be accompanied by adults, and you might want to provide something for them to eat. I don't think it's necessarily expected, and usually there is more than enough of the children's food for the adults to pick at. A cup of tea is always welcome though. Some people like to offer a glass of wine: it can be much appreciated when adults arrive to pick up older children in the early evening, but do be aware of not giving too much to drivers.

THE CAKE

If you are making your own cake it doesn't matter how amateur looking it is or how strange tasting – your child will be delighted that you did it just for him. Choose a personal theme – there's no point in struggling to make a cake that looks as if it has

LEFT: *Two 'cakes' made by my four-year-old that he insisted I include. Just in case you're not sure they are 'two snakes' and 'eggs and a lot of sausages'. Never forget you may have a budding cake designer in your midst.*
BELOW: *No, these aren't ice creams – they're cakes! (see page 92).*

come from a shop. Don't make it too big – the children will be full of food and will only want a small piece. I have made cakes with ice-cream inside them for the last few parties and they've gone down extremely well; much better than the rich chocolate or jam sponge ones used to.

If you would rather buy one then do order it in plenty of time. Tell them exactly what you want – don't be bullied into having one of their standard lines – and don't let them make an enormous one which will only be half eaten.

SHOPPING LIST

It may be useful to check some of these off as the party approaches:

Invitations	☐	Equipment for games	☐
Paper cloths	☐	Prizes	☐
Paper napkins	☐	Going home bags and contents	☐
Paper plates, beakers and bowls	☐	Food for children	☐
Cutlery	☐	Food for adults	☐
Crackers	☐	Drink for children	☐
Balloons	☐	Drink for adults	☐
Cake candles	☐	Cake ingredients	☐
Decorations	☐		

CHECK LIST

Four Weeks Ahead
1   Make list of children to invite.   ☐
2   Decide on date, time and place for party.   ☐
3   Start family discussions on food to be served.   ☐
4   Think about a theme.   ☐
5   Have you booked an entertainer if necessary?   ☐
6   Start thinking of games, for when they arrive and before and after the meal.   ☐
7   Have you got an idea for the cake or have you ordered one?   ☐
8   Do you need anyone to help?   ☐

One Week Ahead
1   Have you telephoned the parents who haven't replied?   ☐
2   Make sure that your reservation is confirmed if you're having the party
    outside the house.   ☐
3   Do you have some way of playing music for games?   ☐
4   Make sure someone will have a camera and film to record the party.   ☐

The Day Before
1   Has the birthday cake been made or collected?   ☐
2   Get the going home bags filled and ready.   ☐
3   Has all the food been bought? And drinks, crisps, etc?   ☐
4   Are the games prepared – pass the parcel wrapped etc?   ☐
5   Prepare the food as much as possible.   ☐

The Day of the Party
1   Have you put balloons on the front door?   □
2   Is the party space cleared, everything breakable removed?   □
3   Have you put away any precious toys?   □
4   Plenty of lavatory paper?   □
5   Any pets safely out of the way?   □
6   Is the table laid?   □

THE GREAT DAY

Preparing the Birthday Person

It's easy for the star of the day, particularly if very young, to get over-excited and become grizzly, temperamental and difficult. Try not to do anything too frantic during the lead-up to the party – keep it very low-key and calm (if you can during your last minute hectic preparations!) One of ours threw a terrible tantrum on his second birthday and almost made the whole event a misery. If the birthday person does play up, avoid the temptation to make remarks like 'All the trouble I've taken and you're spoiling everything' or 'I've worked my fingers to the bone and you've GOT TO HAVE A GOOD TIME!' Try to keep smiling and remember that the mood will pass . . . (well, by the time he's twenty-one anyway . . .)

Preparing the Party Room

Ideally you should have one room for games and one for the meal, but if that's not possible at least try to clear a reasonably large area for playing games. Push back the sofas and chairs (or the bed, if you're using the bedroom), clear away any precious or breakable objects and check carefully for safety. Never have an open fire and make sure all heaters have the correct guards. Check for safety of electric sockets, for loose wires, small objects that could be choked on or anything poisonous like cleaning fluid or alcohol that could be reached by an inquisitive child. Keep any dogs or cats well out of the way (for their sake as well as the children's) and cover the floor if it's likely to get easily stained. If you are having an entertainer, clear him a space to work in so he can prepare while you are having the meal.

Laying the Table

It's unwise to sit children on the floor unless you really have to, so it's worth finding enough chairs to seat them all around the table, or better still, getting hold of special little low tables and chairs. You may find your child's nursery school will lend you some, or alternatively you can hire them from party shops (see page 125).

    They make some beautiful, colourful paper cloths, plates and cups nowadays, and it's a treat to be able to throw everything away at the end of the party and not worry about washing up. You don't have to buy the very expensive ones with pictures of TV or cartoon characters on them – the plain ones are much cheaper. If you get white ones you could decorate the cups with felt tip patterns or stuck on shapes. A white paper cloth can also be drawn on, or decorated with cut-outs stapled on to it. Paper is a bit wasteful, however, and a plastic cloth can at least be wiped and used again. Don't use

TOP: Paper plates decorated with felt tips, stickers and coloured tape. LEFT: A white paper cloth can be decorated the same way. RIGHT: Or get a young artist to draw on it!

real glasses for children, and certainly not your best china.

Place names are a waste of time for very young children, but as the birthday person gets older he/she may have very firm ideas about who sits where, and ready-named positions can save a lot of arguing. Crackers, streamers, noisy blowers and paper hats all add to the fun. If it's a large party you may want to wait to distribute the crackers and blowers until the end of the meal, as otherwise it can get very chaotic.

As they Arrive

It's important to have something planned for the guests to do as soon as they walk in the door, otherwise you're very likely to find yourself with shy, uneasy children hanging around silently in corners. It's certainly no good assuming you can throw a group of similarly-aged children together and they will automatically play and chat. I know how I feel when walking into a roomful of adults at a drinks party; it's only because I've learnt to pretend that I'm at ease that *I* don't stand silently in a corner.

You need to have something very simple and uncompetitive ready for them, and obviously something that doesn't matter being joined in at any stage. You'll find plenty of ideas in the birthday parties section.

Make sure you put coats, hats and gloves somewhere they will be easily found at the end of the party.

It can be great fun to make a video of the party; you can hire a video camera and player reasonably cheaply. If you tape the children one by one as they come in (but make sure they're old enough for it not to make them feel shy) and then play it back towards the end of the party it can cause great giggles, and it's a lovely memento for you to keep.

Games

Once all the guests have arrived you can start your pre-meal games. This is the time for energetic musical games, frantic pass-the-parcels and silly guessing games. Suit the games to the age of the children, and always have a few extra ones planned in case they go more quickly than you expect (although in my experience they tend to take longer). There are bound to be some competitive games, but keep an eye out that no one gets laughed at or left out, and that everyone gets a prize of some sort, however tiny. As the time for the meal approaches, let the games get a bit calmer so the children can cool down and get in the mood for sitting quietly(!) at the table.

The train down (or along, or up) to tea is always very popular. Position the birthday person at the front and join the others behind him/her, all holding the child in front round the waist. On the word go, the train chugs off to the meal, making appropriate noises as it goes.

The train moves off to tea.

The 'pitta beds' for our pyjama party (page 47).

The Meal

If you have place names help the children to find them, and if not try to see that no one is seated next to their worst enemy . . . Make sure everyone has plenty to drink – they may be very thirsty after all those games. Keep passing and offering the sandwiches, biscuits and crisps, and if you're serving hot food let it cool slightly before it is served. Don't worry if some of the children eat very little – they may well be too excited to eat much, and a party is not the time to worry about nutrition. And if table manners are not quite as you would normally expect them to be, let it go. This is a very special day and one to be enjoyed, even if it means letting the guests float crisps on their apple juice to see if they will sink. Only if one guest is about to throttle another should you come really heavy, and watch out for excessive giggles – it's only too easy for children to choke if they laugh while they're eating.

Don't let anyone leave the table until all the children have finished or there'll be chaos. Have a wet flannel ready for hand and mouth de-sticking, and organise trips to the lavatory.

After the Meal

Once everyone is reasonably unsticky and has been to the lavatory, it's time for more games or the organised entertainment. If you are having a professional entertainer help him to sit the children where they can all see but where they're not so near that they will keep fiddling with his props! Clear all toys well away – as a performer myself I often feel for a magic man who is valiantly struggling to keep his audience's attention while they are being tempted away by their host's motorbike or Thundertank. Try to organise it so that the entertainment or games will be finished well before the pick-up

Playing 'thimbles'; have plenty of games lined up so there are no awkward pauses.

time, as it can be very frustrating for parents who are in a hurry to have to battle with a screaming child who is missing the end of Punch and Judy or the dramatic appearance of the white rabbit out of the hat. When I was a child we used often to be given jelly and ice-cream at the end of a party; it was a good way of calming everything down and getting everyone into one place. Mind you, there were no such things as going home bags then, so I suppose it was partly an end-of-party treat.

Going Home

Make sure someone is on hand when the doorbell starts ringing to hand out coats, going home bags and balloons. It may be rather acquisitive that children now assume they will be getting something as they go, but it does seem to have become an established tradition. It also eases the departure, as most children will be only too happy to put on their coats if they know there is something to gain at the end of it . . . You can either buy little decorated plastic bags or just plain paper bags decorated with felt tip or stickers, and the 'goodies' inside needn't be anything expensive – just tiny little toys, pretty rubbers or little paper books. Scout around your local newsagents and toy shops, or try a small mail order firm or two, who may supply a large bag of little things very cheaply.

Either buy going home bags or make your own.

Finale

Some people like to offer the adults a glass of wine and a nibble or two as they come to pick up the children. If you do, then see that there is still something for the children to play while they are waiting. I think it all depends on the age of the children and the type of party as to whether you will feel like being this hospitable: I must admit by the time the party is over I am usually quite pleased to see everyone go and have the house to ourselves again.

When all is quiet, let the birthday person open his presents (or there may be a special friend or two he/she would like to stay behind and watch). Write down who gave what so that you can try the impossible task of encouraging the receiver to grudgingly write the thank you letters, or so that you can do them if he/she is too young. (Or so that you can *think* you're going to do them, and mean to do them but if you're like me . . .) After the party there may well be a sense of anti-climax so give the birthday person lots of love and let him/her stay up a little later than usual to talk over with the family the wonderful party that you've all had.

A party for the first birthday is very special but is obviously given almost entirely for the benefit of the proud parents and friends. Don't invite more than four to six babies and preferably all roughly the same age: eighteen months and under. Make sure everything is very safe for the children and also that any precious ornaments or easily stained furniture are kept out of the way. Try to make the room play-proof.

Lucy at her first birthday party with the simplest cake of all – a cupcake with a candle in it. In the bowl are our homemade rusks.

ook a basket and her umbrella, and

A lovely cake for a first birthday and very simple to make.

TIME

Don't have it too long as babies of this age tire very quickly. Most of them will probably have an afternoon nap, so you must work around that, and it could be that some of them also sleep in the morning. Check this before you arrange a definite time. Any of the following are suitable:

Coffee time 11.30 to 12.30
Lunch 12.30 to 1.30
or after the afternoon sleep at 4.00 to 5.00

PLACE

Home almost certainly – you have potties, changing table, familiar surroundings and so on. You won't need much room and you'll feel much more relaxed.

THEME

The birthday person is of course too young to appreciate a theme, but if you want to make everything all pink or blue or covered in little bows why not? I know when my children were that young I could hardly find time to get myself dressed, let alone do anything else – but you may be more organised than I was, or have a less demanding baby (are there such things?)

ENTERTAINMENT

This too can be minimal. Pile all the toys in the middle of the room – but nothing the birthday person is particularly possessive about (if that leaves you with none at all you'll just have to borrow). Tearing up old newspapers or tissue paper can cause great enjoyment, a few saucepans with spoons to bang, old handbags full of interesting objects and some music to 'sing' and dance to. If it's warm you could set out a bowl of water and some toys to float in it, but only do it where you can protect the surroundings. Don't force the children into anything – just let them potter about, as long as you're watching their safety all the time.

Do remember to take lots of photographs or hire a video camera. The memories of a first birthday are very precious.

FOOD

Most important of all is the safety of the children's food – don't have any nuts (I hope you don't have them around in any case), pieces of apple, raisins or sweets. The babies will need very little to eat, but if you're giving the party at lunch time you should try to provide some sort of food for the grown ups. (But if you can't, *don't worry*, everyone understands the strain of looking after a young baby.)

THE CAKE

It really isn't worth spending hours on a complicated cake – even a candle stuck into a doughnut or cupcake will mark the occasion – or try our very simple but symbolic candle cake. There will be only too many occasions in the years to come when you will be begged to produce all sorts of challenging masterpieces!

For the adults – chicken breast with tomato and mozzarella, apple orange snow.
ABOVE: *For the babies – purée or sieve the chicken, tomato and mozzarella, adding a little liquid if necessary. The apple orange snow is perfect for them, but without the fruit garnish.*

Menu 1

Coffee time

Homemade rusks
Coffee cake (for adults)
Coffee (for adults)

Menu 2

Lunch

Chicken breast with tomato sauce,
mozzarella and herb garnish (for adults
and puréed for the babies)
Apple orange snow

AGE 2

This is the start of the notorious 'terrible twos' – some children seem to sail through them with a charming smile, but more usually it is the age of the tantrum. Certainly all of my children have been through some monumental protests, and unfortunately the excitement and tension of the birthday festivities can be the trigger for setting one off. It's impossible to forestall all possible causes – it's likely to be something as serious as the fact you've put the wrong colour socks on him/her. Don't be depressed if there is a bit of a tantrum – keep it calm and it'll pass . . .

Any fancy dress must be very comfortable like these soft animal headdresses.

TIME AND PLACE

As for age 1, because there may still be many of the guests who have a daytime nap or two. As you won't need a lot of room, home is still the most relaxed place to have it unless there is any good reason against it.

NUMBERS

Not too many; at this age children get easily overwhelmed by a sea of faces. I would suggest between three and eight guests. All the accompanying adults will stay, so you should have plenty of help.

THEMES

At this age children begin to have very definite likes and dislikes, so there'll probably be something that will immediately come to mind when planning the party. I've picked ANIMALS as a theme, as most little ones seem very keen on them. I wouldn't really bother to decorate the room too much unless you particularly want to, as two-year-olds are generally more interested in tiny details than grand designs. If they feel like dressing up make sure the costumes are extremely comfortable and easy to remove during the party. Don't take too much trouble making them: if the

The bold cat's head cake.

pussy cat rebels and wants to wear a party frock you don't want to have wasted hours of work. Do something like our easy headdresses.

ENTERTAINMENT

Keep the games simple. Children of this age don't need highly organised games to make them happy. You could hire a (very gentle) clown if you want to, but I really don't think it's worth the expense. They will be just as happy with some of the following:

As they arrive
DRAWING AND COLOURING
Provide lots of big sheets of paper and crayons, and perhaps some gummed stickers.

Before and after the meal
MUSICAL BUMPS
Use a radio or cassette player, preferably with a tape of nursery rhymes or other music that the children will enjoy. Persuade them to dance about while the music is playing, then to sit down when the music stops. Whoever is last to sit down goes out, until there is only one child left, who wins the game. If they refuse to stop dancing when they're out then so be it. I don't think rules have to be enforced at the age of two. Have a little prize for the winner, and perhaps further prizes for the 'best dancer', 'prettiest dress', 'shiniest shoes' and so on, until . . . surprise surprise – everyone wins something!

PLAYING WITH BALLOONS
Can cause endless amusement. Just have plenty of large, colourful balloons and keep throwing them up in the air and letting the children pat them about.

RING-A-RING-A-ROSES
A good old favourite. All join hands in a circle and sing:

      Ring-a-ring-a-roses
      A pocket full of posies
      A-tishoo A-tishoo
      We all fall down.

Everyone falls down on the last phrase. Repeat as often as you wish.

HERE WE GO ROUND THE MULBERRY BUSH
Again stand in a circle; join hands and dance round in a circle, singing:

> Here we go round the mulberry bush,
> The mulberry bush, the mulberry bush
> Here we go round the mulberry bush
> On a cold and frosty morning.

Each of the verses describes some everyday action, which you mime while standing still:

> This is the way we wash our hands,
> Wash our hands, wash our hands,
> This is the way we wash our hands
> On a cold and frosty morning.

Then join hands again and dance round singing the chorus. Further verses can be anything from 'brush our hair' to 'sweep the floor', and can continue as long as everyone is still enjoying themselves.

ANIMAL NOISES
Ask the children 'Who can make the noise of a cow? a sheep?' etc. Endless fun.

PUPPET SHOW
You might consider organising a very simple puppet show, using some of the birthday person's teddies and toys. Just squatting behind a sofa and moving them about and making them wave hello and talk to the children can cause immense pleasure. If there's an older sibling this could be a very good job for them to do.

FOOD

Still be aware of safety, and make it look very colourful and inviting. Beg or borrow enough high chairs and booster seats for all, or hire or borrow little tables and chairs. Don't give them too much food, and serve small portions.

As with age 1, you might want to provide a little something for the adults to eat and drink.

THE CAKE

Choose something bold and easily recognisable, like our easy pussy cat face.

The lunch-time menu: Home made strawberry ice cream and brown rice with bolognese sauce, both easy to eat and very popular.

The animal tea. CLOCKWISE FROM BOTTOM LEFT: *yoghurt and honey lollies, iced animal-shaped biscuits, goldfish jelly, animal-shaped sandwiches.*

Menu 1

Tea or coffee time

Animal-shaped sandwiches
Animal-shaped biscuits
Yoghourt and honey lollies
Goldfish jelly

Menu 2

Lunch

Brown rice and bolognese sauce
Strawberry ice cream

AGE 3

Now they're really getting into socialising! Your birthday person may be attending some sort of playgroup or nursery school by now, so he/she may know exactly which friends are wanted. Months can make a difference, so try to invite children not too far apart in ages; two and a half is very different from three for instance.

Tom and Georges brought their favourite friends along to the dolls' and teddies' tea party, and my ancient teddy, Oswald, joined in. This tea is a lovely excuse to make pretty, miniature food, and some of the guests will be wonderfully well-behaved . . .

The three bears' cake is very suitable for the nursery rhyme theme, or for any three-year-old party.

TIME AND PLACE

You could extend the length of the party to one-and-a-quarter hours at this stage. A lunch time party can be fun, but still check for afternoon naps, and some may attend morning or afternoon school. Consider:

12.00 to 1.15
3.30 to 4.45

Home is still the easiest and most relaxing, but you will need a bit more room for games. If you need the living room for tea, don't forget the bedroom: it can make a good space for games if you push the furniture against the walls. If you don't feel you've got enough room, perhaps a friend lives somewhere suitable that you could borrow?

NUMBERS

Depending on the character of the birthday person and the number of friends they want to include, I suggest not more than eight to twelve.

THEMES

There are probably lots of things that spring to mind – favourite television characters, Disney,

zoos, circuses and so on. Here are a couple of suggestions:

1   Nursery Rhymes
This gives you great scope. Either choose a particular favourite or mix several. Ask the guests to come in some sort of simple costume of

Mary Mary's costume, you'd never know it was made mostly from paper! (See also page 6.)

a nursery rhyme character. Our Mary, Mary costume is particularly easy and cheap – all the frills are made from lavatory paper! (Make extra sure of fire precautions when any of the children is wearing anything made of paper.)

2 Dolls' and Teddies' Tea Party

Ask all the guests to bring their favourite doll or teddy, and lay a place for them as well as for their human owners. Have little prizes ready for the dolls as well as the children. If the birthday person was given a doll or teddy when he/she was born then it will be the doll's birthday too and you can make it a double celebration.

The 'Humpty Dumpty' eggs.

The dolls' and teddies' tea – everything in miniature.

ENTERTAINMENT

As they arrive

MODELLING

Have plenty of flour and water dough ready. Let them make any shapes they fancy, and while the party is running dry the shapes out in a low oven so they can take home their 'sculptures'.

Before and after the meal

PASS THE PARCEL

This is the age to start Pass-the-parcel. The day before the party, wrap a small present in paper (it can be newspaper, it needn't be expensive wrapping paper). Wrap it in layer after layer of paper, but *between every layer put a tiny present or sweet*. Sit the children in a circle on the floor and play some music. They must pass the parcel from hand to hand until the music stops, when whoever is holding the parcel can take off one layer, keeping whatever goody falls out. Make sure everyone gets a go. Whoever opens the last layer gets the present.

MUSICAL BUMPS AND STATUES

As for age 2, but add musical statues, in which the children have to stand still when the music stops. Any wobbling and they're out.

FOLLOW MY LEADER

Very simple but very popular. One child is the leader and everyone else follows behind him/her doing exactly what the leader does – hopping, skipping, making funny noises etc.

A professional magic man or clown is well worth considering at this age for an hour or so's entertainment after the meal. The home-made puppet show as for age 2 would still go down well.

FOOD

If you are feeding the adults they will still have to eat in the same room.

THE CAKE

Our 'Mary Mary Quite Contrary' makes a lovely centrepiece, and is almost a meal in itself: the children can pick at the sweet and savoury things growing in her 'garden'. For the dolls' and teddies' tea make a tiny cake to go with the miniature food.

The Mary Mary cake – sweet and savoury all in one centrepiece.

Menu 1

Nursery rhyme tea or lunch

'Humpty Dumpty' scrambled eggs
Pig-shaped sandwiches
('This little piggy went to market . . .')
Star-shaped biscuits

Menu 2

Dolls' and teddies' tea

Mini sandwiches
Mini scotch pancakes
Mini cheese scones
Mini pink meringues
Mini biscuits
Chocolate animals

Children are really getting into the birthday party circuit by now and will probably have quite definite ideas of what they want. Do listen to them – if the birthday person wants a green striped cake then he/she must have one. Most guests will stay alone at this age, so you'll have fewer adults around and may need to organise someone to help. Don't ever force a child to stay on his own – apart from it being unkind, you certainly don't want to get landed with a crying guest while you're trying to run the party.

The pink and pretty tea – everything as frilly and feminine as possible.
CLOCKWISE FROM BOTTOM: heart-shaped sandwiches, pink milkshake jelly, pink biscuits and glacé strawberries.

Thomas cake and macaroni cheese with sausage boats.

More transport: the aeroplane jelly.

TIME AND PLACE

Tea time is the most traditional and probably most popular, but lunch can still be a possibility, as the children will not yet be at full time school, and may get less tired at a midday party.
12.00 to 1.30
3.00 to 4.30

Home or a friend's house is the best, but the games may get quite energetic and if you're having large numbers you might need to consider hiring a room in a hotel or local church hall or playschool.

NUMBERS

As they're getting much more civilised now you can probably accommodate between ten and fifteen children, but I wouldn't go beyond that. If the birthday person is at a shy stage, you may want to keep it smaller.

THEMES

1   A pretty tea
Make everything very pink and frilly and ask the guests to wear their best party outfits. You don't have to spend a fortune to make a beautiful dress – ours was made from a vest and remnants off a market stall, and is very easy to do.

2   Transport
Very popular and offering endless scope. If there is a particular favourite type of transport like an aeroplane or a car, then you could base everything around it, or just have a jolly mix, as we have.

Our easy-to-make pretty pink party dress.

ENTERTAINMENT

As they arrive

Before the party, cut some bright picture post-cards in half (or you could use magazine pictures, but it's worth pasting them on to card). Hide the halves around the room or the hallway and as each child arrives, give them a half picture and ask them to find the other half. Have ready tiny prizes (perhaps badges, or paper hats) ready to give them as they find their missing pieces.

Before and after the meal

MUSICAL STATUES

See page 34, but you can add elaborations. When the music stops everyone must pretend to be an animal, or to be cross, or happy etc.

ORANGES AND LEMONS

A lovely old game, which still causes great pleasure. Either two adults or two of the tallest children form an arch by joining hands and holding their arms up high. One of them is an orange and one a lemon (I should make the decision for them, or you could be involved in hours of heavy negotiations) but none of the other children must know which is which. The other children form a chain by holding on to the waist of the player in front, and everyone sings 'Oranges and Lemons' as the chain passes round and round through the arch. When the word 'HEAD' is reached the arch drops its arms and catches the child passing underneath, who is asked secretly whether he/she wants to be an Orange or a Lemon. Having decided, the child holds on to that side of the arch round the waist, and the song begins again.

Here is the song (there is a much longer version, but I think this is quite long enough to keep everyone happy):

'Oranges and lemons,'
Say the bells of St Clement's
'You owe me five farthings,'
Say the bells of St Martin's.
'When will you pay me?'
Say the bells of Old Bailey.
'When I grow rich,'
Say the bells of Shoreditch.
'When will that be?'

Some of the old games are still popular: here the girls are playing oranges and lemons.

Say the bells of Stepney.
'I do not know,'
Says the great bell of Bow.
'Here comes a candle to light you to bed
Here comes a chopper to
CHOP OFF YOUR HEAD!'

WHAT'S THE TIME, MR WOLF?

One child is the wolf (or it could be a grown-up). The other children stand on the other side of the room then try to creep up on the wolf when his back is turned. He can turn to face them whenever he likes, and they must immediately stand still and ask 'What's the time, Mr Wolf?' The wolf can either choose to answer 3 o'clock, 4 o'clock and so on and then turn back, or to shout 'DINNER TIME!' when he runs to the children and tries to catch one. This game is enormous fun, but do watch that no one gets too scared by the tension of the wolf's feeding habits!

PASS THE PARCEL

See page 34, but instead of just sweets or toys in every layer you can add simple forfeits written on slips of paper, such as 'bark like a dog', 'hop on one foot' and so on.

PIN THE TAIL ON THE DONKEY

Trace or draw a donkey (minus tail) on a large sheet of paper and stick it to the wall (with blu-tack or something similar). If you want to be more elaborate and glue it on to a sheet of hardboard so much the better – you will at least be able to use it again for future parties. The object of the game is for each child to try and stick his tail in place while blindfolded. It's usual to make just one tail, but I think it's quite fun to make one for each child, cut out of paper, so at the end you can see where all the tails have landed up. Blindfold each child (a paper mask with padding stuck to the inside is a comfortable way of doing it, or woolly hat pulled down over the eyes), hand him/her a tail with a blob of blu-tack on the top then point him/her in the right direction. You'll end up with tails growing all over the place; whoever gets nearest wins a tiny prize.

THE FARMYARD

This needs an adult who is good at making up stories. He (or she) tells each child which farm-yard animal he/she is going to be: Simon will be a pig, Lucy a sheep and so on. The grown up

Another transport cake: the ever popular Postman Pat.

Putting icing onto biscuits makes them very elegant.

tells a story about life in the farmyard, and every time an animal is mentioned, however briefly, the right child must make the noise of that animal. Whenever the storyteller says 'And all the animals woke up!' they must *all* make their noises together!

ENTERTAINER

A magician is really appreciated at this age, so even if you can't afford to hire a professional entertainer, perhaps there's an uncle or grand-father who could be persuaded to do a few tricks?

THE CAKE

Menu 1
You need a really pretty cake. This pink My Little Pony cake is perfect.

Menu 2
Choose your birthday person's favourite vehicle – Thomas the Tank Engine and Postman Pat's van are just two possibilities.

Menu 1

A pretty tea

Heart-shaped sandwiches
Pink biscuits
Whole glacé strawberries
Pink milk shake jelly

Menu 2

A transport lunch

Macaroni cheese
(served with toast or fried bread boats)
Sausage sailing boats
Aeroplane jelly

AGE 5

This is a great age for parties. They are not remotely toddlers any more by now – they are real children. A party for this age group needs proper organising or it can easily become chaotic. The birthday person may well be in a 'sexist' phase by now and find the whole idea of boys or girls boring or soppy. It's best to give in to it at this stage and have an all-masculine or all-feminine party if so desired.

What is the group name for this impressive collection? A save of superheroes perhaps . . . LEFT TO RIGHT: *Philip as He-Man, Jack as Mr T, Marc as Superman, Adam as Batman, Dominic as Spider-Man.* BELOW: *Emily as She-Ra.*

TIME AND PLACE

The party may have to be after school, so perhaps 4.00 to 5.30 might be a good time. Friday may be a good day to have it if the children are too tired during the week, or at the weekend. If the birthday falls in the holidays, do make sure all the friends are not going to be away – it may be necessary to have the party near to the beginning or end of term. A lunch party can be a very good idea at weekends or

The easy to make costumes. TOP ROW LEFT TO RIGHT: Superman, He-Man, Spider-Man. BOTTOM ROW LEFT TO RIGHT: Mr T, Batman, She-Ra.

in the holidays. If you're inviting large numbers you may need to hire somewhere outside – you don't want hordes of schoolchildren crammed into your living room. Also if it's the right time of year, outside parties are great fun (see page 86).

NUMBERS

If the birthday person has started school you may need to invite the whole class, but don't be shamed into it if he/she doesn't want all of them. Twelve to fifteen is a good number.

THEMES

1   Superheroes
The perfect age for this. Ask the guests to come as the superhero of their choice (at my son's fifth birthday we had six Spider-Men!). You can simply make our costumes, or there are ready-made ones you can buy.

2   School
The birthday person may be very proud of being at 'big school' and if the party is straight after school nobody will have to change out of school uniform, if there is one.

ENTERTAINMENT

As they arrive
THE GREEN PENNIES
Hide 250 pence, which you have previously sprayed bright green, all over the house or room. As the children arrive, give them a little bag and tell them to find as many as they can. At the end of the party, whoever has the most gets a little prize. (Keep the pennies to use for another party, or for gambling with for card games!)

Before and after the meal
SIMPLE SIMON
An old favourite. All the children stand facing a grown-up, who tells them various things to do like 'Simple Simon says put your hands in the air', 'Simple Simon says touch your toes' and so on. They must only do as requested *if* it is prefaced by 'Simple Simon says', so if the adult just says 'Touch your toes' they must *not* do it. Make it faster and faster and the instructions sillier and sillier. Anyone who obeys an instruction without 'Simon says' in front of it is out.

MUSICAL CHAIRS
Place a line of chairs down the middle of the room. They should face alternate ways, and there must be one less chair than the number of players. When the music starts the children dance round and round the chairs (and they must keep moving, not hover over a chair), and when the music stops they must find a chair to sit on. Each time there will be one player left without a chair, who is then out. Take away a chair and start again, until finally there are just two children dancing round one chair. Whoever gets it is the winner.

SWEET BASHING
Fill a strong brown paper bag with sweets and string it up quite high where the children can just reach it with a stick. The children take it in turns to hit the bag with the stick until it breaks and the sweets come falling out, when everyone scrambles to get some!

MUSICAL STATUES
See page 34, but add more sophisticated elaborations (when the music stops everyone must be something beginning with W, and so on).

PASS THE PARCEL
See page 34, but put trickier forfeits between the layers (spell your name, pretend to be like your teacher, etc).

The ever popular pass the parcel.

TREASURE HUNT

Divide the children into two teams. Have clues ready for each team; these should be drawn in pictures and very easy, and describe where the next clue is. Draw one team's clues in red and one in green so they don't pick up the wrong one, and position them in the opposite order so they're not chasing after the same one and following each other around. The last clue (for both teams) should lead to the treasure.

DEAD LIONS

A lovely quiet game, and surprisingly popular. Good to play towards the end of the party or just before tea when you want to quieten things down a bit. The children have to lie on the floor and not move a muscle: a grown up has to try to make them move by whatever means he likes, but without touching them. Such tricks as 'Johnny, your mother's come to collect you', or 'Susan, there's a fly crawling up your nose' are all quite acceptable. If they move or giggle they are out.

SARDINES

Just like hide and seek, but as soon as anyone finds the hidden person they must hide with

ABOVE: The school book cake. BELOW: Spider-Man climbing a wall, a good cake for the superhero theme.

CLOCKWISE FROM LEFT: vanilla ice cream with Spider-Man sauce, Superman cake, Mini toads-in-the-hole with homemade baked beans.

them, until finally there is just one person looking and everyone else crammed into a corner trying not to laugh!

FLOATING FEATHER
All the players form a circle. A feather is held above the centre of the circle and the players have to try to keep it afloat as long as possible by blowing as hard as they can. No winners, just fun.

ON AND OFF THE BLANKET
A very exciting and exhausting game. Spread a large old blanket on the floor in the middle of the room. Tell the players to stand on the blanket and then issue them with instructions, to which *they must do the opposite*. Thus, when you say 'Everyone off the blanket' they must all stay on it, and when you say 'Everyone on the blanket' they must get off. Start slowly and build up the pace and excitement. Anyone who makes

the wrong move is out, until only one person is left.

Hop Rabbit Hop

A bit like musical statues, but sillier. Begin by asking all the children to think of a rabbit name, and it must be one you consider suitably rabbity – such as Hoppy, Flopsy, Thumper, Bunny etc. Names such as Bernard, Fiona or Charlemagne don't qualify. When they've all chosen their names get them to squat down and hop about, holding their knees. When you shout 'STOP!' they must all keep completely still exactly as they are for ten seconds, until you say 'HOP RABBIT HOP!' when they must start hopping again. Any rabbit who wobbles or carries on hopping after you have said 'STOP!' is out. The last rabbit left wins the prize (perhaps a carrot!)

THE CAKE

Menu 1
Choose your favourite superhero – we've done Superman and Spider-Man.

Menu 2
A school book is easy and very suitable.

Menu 1

Superheroes

Mini toads-in-the-hole
Homemade baked beans
Vanilla ice cream and Spider-Man sauce

Menu 2

School

Mini shepherd's pies
Homemade baked beans
Chocolate nut squares and custard

Still in the peak of party appreciation. The party will have been talked about, thought about and looked forward to for weeks – perhaps months! (My son started planning his next birthday the day after his last one was over . . .) Listen carefully to what is requested, as the birthday person will have a very clear idea of what he/she wants.

3 *Left-over Christmas decorations on jumble sale hat.*
4 *Pasta glued on plastic bowler.*
5 *Plastic hat, J-cloth rose, scourer leaves.*
6 *Sweets stuck on paper bowl.*
7 *Hats glued in a pile.*

The hats' party.
1 *Foil bowl, scourer and red nose.*
2 *Paper bowls trimmed with string and artificial flowers.*

TIME AND PLACE

The same times apply as for age 5 (page 41). You might like to consider an outing of some kind at this age (see page 127) or at least hire a large room so they can all let off steam. If you feel you have a large enough room at home, so much the better, but make it clear which rooms are out of bounds.

NUMBERS

You're into big parties now! Don't have less than twelve, and go up to eighteen or twenty or more if you can.

ABOVE: children dressed for the pyjama party – with the table made to look like a bed. BELOW: James and Louise decorating bags.

THEMES

There may not be time for serious dressing up because of school, but you can still have a bit of fun.

1   Hats and Headdresses
Ask them all to come in some sort of headgear – as silly as they like.

2   Pyjama Party
Very popular and easy – everyone comes wearing pyjamas.

ENTERTAINMENT

All of the games given for age 5 are suitable or some or all of the following:

As they arrive
DECORATING BAGS
Have ready enough plain white paper bags for every child (I begged some from my local newsagent). Spread out lots of stickers, labels, felt tips, ribbons, bows, sellotape and so on. Give the children a bag each and let them decorate them as they wish, including writing their names on – these will be the going home bags at the end of the party.

Before and after the meal
HOKEY COKEY
All the children stand in a circle. They sing and do the actions to the following:
>   You put your right hand in (*to the circle*)
>   Your right hand out
>   In, out, in, out
>   Shake it all about
>   You do the Hokey-cokey (*sort of wiggle from side to side*)

And you turn around.
That's what it's all about.
All the children join hands for the chorus:

> Oh Hokey Cokey Cokey
> (*all move together
> into the middle of the circle*)
> Oh Hokey Cokey Cokey
> (*all move back as far as
> possible, still holding hands*)
> Oh Hokey Cokey Cokey
> (*all in again*)
> Knees bend, arms stretch
> Ra Ra Ra!
> (*let go of hands and do the
> actions*).

The verses thereafter use:

> Your left hand
> Your right foot
> Your left foot
> Your right arm
> Your left arm
> Your right leg
> Your left leg
> Your head
> Your whole self (*the players have to jump in
> and out of the circle*).

*Lamb burger hats with mixed vegetables; raspberry ice cream with
gingerbread men.*

HUNT THE THIMBLE

One of the oldest of English games – invented several hundred years ago. Send everyone out of the room, then 'hide' a thimble. Not out of sight – you must be able to find it without moving anything. When the children come back in, they must hunt the thimble, and when someone finds it he must say absolutely nothing, but sit down on the floor with his arms folded. The game continues until all the children are sitting down except one. He is the loser, and must hide the thimble for the next round.

TREASURE HUNT

As for age 5, but written clues rather than drawings.

FIND MY CHILD

You must pretend to be a parent who has lost a child in a large department store. One of the children is a detective and you must ask the detecive to find the missing child. In describing the child to the detective you, of course, describe one of the other children playing the game and the fun is to see how quickly the detective works out which is 'your' child. You can make your descriptions as cryptic or easy as you like, and once the child is guessed, choose another detective and another 'lost' child.

THROWING THE HANKY

A very simple game, but it can get very exciting. All the players but one sit in a circle. The one who is left stands in the middle. Give one of the seated players a rolled up hanky which he must throw to another player opposite. The one in the middle must try to catch the hanky as it flies past. When he does, he changes places with the player who last threw it.

SAUSAGES

A very silly game indeed, which is why it's such fun. A victim is chosen and the others then fire all sorts of ridiculous and personal questions at him. 'What's your favourite subject at school?' 'How old are you?' 'Who's your best friend?' and so on. To all these questions the victim must answer 'SAUSAGES!' and keep a straight face. The moment he giggles or even smiles, he is out, and someone else takes his place.

THE CAKE

Menu 1
A hat cake is easy to make.
Menu 2
Anything to do with pyjamas or sleep would be good – I've chosen the Seven Dwarfs asleep in bed.

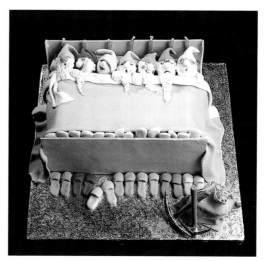

ABOVE LEFT: chocolate clusters, muesli bars and pitta beds. ABOVE RIGHT: the Seven Dwarfs' cake. BELOW: Hat cake.

Menu 1	**Menu 2**
Hats	*Pyjama Party*
Lamb burger hats with mixed vegetables	Filled pitta (pitta beds!)
Raspberry ice-cream	Muesli bars
Iced gingerbread men	Chocolate clusters

AGE 7

The birthday person will be beginning to feel very grown-up now
Listen carefully to his/her views.

*Paper plates and balloons can easily be decorated with felt tips to follow your theme.
We even found some black paper plates and cups which look very suitably piratey:
Alexander, Maya, Perrine and Holly look very effective in the simplest of costumes.*

Our royals: left to right: Maya as Queen Elizabeth II, Alexander as Henry VIII, Lydia as a Tudor princess, Perrine as King of Diamonds, and Holly as another princess. The background is decorated with gathered paper tablecloths.

TOP: Draw something horsey onto the scarf with felt tips (I cheated and had help – a Scarfe scarf . . .)
BELOW: Biscuits decorated with a little icing.

TIME AND PLACE

It could be exciting to have the party a little later than the previous year – perhaps 5 until 7? You'll almost certainly have to have it at the weekend or in the holidays, as homework will have become a part of weekday evenings, and it would be too tiring in any case to have a party with school the next day. The choice of where to have it depends largely on the numbers – and think hard about an outing.

NUMBERS

It's possible he/she may want to invite just a small select circle of friends, rather than the whole form.

THEMES

1   Royal Tea (or could be spelt Royalty I suppose . . .)

Ask the guests to dress up as something royal. If they don't want to wear anything elaborate then just a gesture (a crown or a sceptre) will do. Spread as much glitter round the house as you can – gold doyleys, 'jewel' sweets, red ribbons etc.

2   Pirate Party

Ask the children to dress very simply as pirates – scarves, earrings, eye patches, swords etc. Hang a few skulls and crossbones around.

ENTERTAINMENT

As they arrive

DECORATING CROWNS

Exactly as for 'decorating bags', but provide them with plain white crowns (not yet joined into circles) cut out of thin card. Staple them to fit when they are finished, and give them to the children when they go home.

Before and after the meal

RING ON A STRING

Take a long piece of string, thread it through a small curtain ring and tie it into a circle. Ask the players to stand in a circle, holding the string in their hands, with one player left in the middle. On the word 'GO' the players must run the string quickly through their hands, hiding the ring as it goes round. The player in the middle must try to guess where the ring is. As he points to a hand, that hand must immediately be lifted up: if the ring is there he changes place with the person in the middle.

MUSICAL NUMBERS

As the music plays, everyone dances about. The moment it stops the umpire shouts out 'Twos', 'Threes', 'Fours', 'Sixes', or any other grouping he fancies. The players have to rush into groups of that number; anyone without a group to go to is out.

SMARTIES WITH STRAWS

Very silly and great fun. Have a pile of Smarties, a bowl and a straw ready. The object is to get as many Smarties as possible into the bowl by sucking them on to the end of the straw and letting them drop into the bowl. You can either do it against the clock, or have a race, and in any case the competitors are of course allowed to eat the Smarties they have moved.

THIMBLES ON TO NAILS

Hammer some nails into a thick piece of wood about 8 in (20 cm) square. Have ready a large bowl of thimbles. The player must try to get as many thimbles as possible on to the nails in a certain time. You could have a tournament and give a prize to the overall winner.

QUIZ GAMES

Sometimes this is an age that enjoys some gentle general knowledge games. Give every player some paper and a pencil and ask some easy questions. Make sure no one is made to feel stupid.

SPIN THE PLATE

You need an unbreakable plate. Sit all the players in a circle and give them each a name of a flower (or animal). Make sure they all remember them,

TOP: *Crown cake for the royal tea.*
BELOW: *the Pirate cake.*

and have a list of them yourself. Put the plate in the middle of the circle and call out the name of a flower. The player who has been called must rush into the circle and spin the plate; when he/she has it spinning you call out another name. The first player must go and sit down and the second one rush to catch the plate before it stops spinning, then set it spinning again. Call out another player to catch that one and so on. Anyone who is too late to catch the plate before it stops is out.

The Royal tea: sandwiches cut into hearts and diamonds, Queen of Hearts biscuits, golden apricot ice cream, jewel biscuits.

MUSICAL RUSH

In the middle of the room place a number of small objects (one less than the number of players) and get the players to form a large circle around them and at least 6 feet (2 metres) away from them. When the music plays they all dance around, and as soon as it stops they must rush to pick up something. One player will fail to get anything, and he must go out, taking one object with him. The last one left is the winner.

DO THIS DO THAT

Exactly like Simon Says (page 42) but they must obey only when you say 'DO THIS' not when you say 'DO THAT'. You have to mime the actions for them to copy, and play it faster and faster until only one person is left.

ROYAL COURT

For sixteen players you need four chairs and one pack of cards. Take the Aces, Kings, Queens and Knaves (Jacks) out of a pack of cards. Get the players to stand around the room while you place the sixteen cards face down in the middle of the room. On the word 'GO' the players all rush forwards and pick up a card. The players who pick up the Aces call out the name of their suits and rush to sit down on one of the chairs. The other three players with cards of the same suit follow the player sitting with the Ace and must sit on his/her knee in the correct order. Thus the King must sit on the Ace's knee, the Queen on the King's knee and the Knave on the Queen's. The first team to be properly seated in the correct order has won.

THE CAKE

Menu 1
A Royal Crown.

Menu 2
A skull and crossbones on a black cake is very dramatic. See the Pirate Cake.

Pirate party food: Baked potatoes cut to skull shape, eyes and nose pressed in and painted with black colouring, nuts for teeth, spare ribs crossed below. Baked beans and banana lollies.

Menu 1

Royal Tea

Sandwiches cut into hearts and diamonds

Jewel biscuits
(biscuits with jam centre and decorations)

Queen of Hearts biscuits
(heart-shaped biscuits iced and gilded)

Golden apricot ice cream

Menu 2

Pirate Party

Barbecued spare ribs

Baked potatoes

Baked beans

Banana lollies

AGE 8

Growing bigger and bigger! The birthday person may feel too sophisticated to think about fancy dress of any kind, so I've suggested a couple of ideas that only involve a bit of thought. (He/she'll probably come round to dressing up again later, even if not until his/her teens!)

The red and green tea party: red and green jelly served in orange quarters, red and green iced biscuits, tomato dip with red and green vegetables, avocado dip, red and green popcorn, little red and green cakes, red and green drinks and a spattered red and green cake. Spray pasta bows red and green and make little place names, and try to find red and green paper plates, napkins, cups and cutlery.

TIME AND PLACE

A meal in a restaurant may be much appreciated, but can be expensive. Perhaps a small group to a show or film? This age is responsible enough if you only have a small number to have them in your best room without worrying too much about breakages and so on. A sleep-over party can be great fun – ask the guests to bring their own sleeping bags and let them stay up late (and lie in late in the morning). This kind of party can start at about 6pm and carry on until late the next day.

NUMBERS

Entirely depends on what sort of party you are having. If it's a sleep-over just make sure there is enough room for all the sleeping bags on your living room or bedroom floor!

THEMES

1   Colours
Choose one or two of the birthday person's favourite colours and ask everyone to come dressed accordingly. Decorate the room with some coloured crepe paper or streamers to match.

2   Topsy-turvy Party
Everything must be back to front or upside-down. Ask the guests to dress as backwards as they can, and give the party backwards. As they walk in give them their going home bags and say goodbye. Say hello as they leave, and so on.

ENTERTAINMENT

Games may not be enough unless really well organised. A long treasure hunt is appreciated, with tricky, rhyming clues.

As they arrive
DRAWING ON THE WALLS
Cover a wall with large sheets of paper and provide plenty of large felt markers. Let the graffiti artists loose!

Playing the graffiti game – dressed topsy-turvy!

Before and after the meal

CHARADES
This children's version of a very old game is great fun. Divide the players into two teams. Give one team a two syllable word to act out to the other team – a word such as seaside or football, where each syllable has meaning. The word will be acted out in three short 'scenes'. If the word was armchair, for instance, the first scene would act out the word 'arm' – perhaps some cricketers practising their bowling or feeling the muscles in their arms. The second scene would portray 'chair' – somebody looking for a chair to sit down in, perhaps. No one must speak. The third little scene acts out the whole word.

FACE THROUGH CARD
Paint a large sheet of card or hardboard with a funny body. Cut out a hole where the face should be and prop the hardboard up so that a child can get behind it. Take a photograph of each child with his head sticking through – just like at the seaside.

STRAIGHT FACES
Divide the players into two teams and sit them in two lines facing each other. One team has to try to make the other one laugh, by telling jokes,

'Uncle Jim', who has made my children happy over many years, entertains at the red and green party.

to whom. When they have finished, remove the sheet and see who has guessed the most correctly, then send the other team out to have their turn at the game.

MUSICAL HATS
Just like musical chairs, but the children sit in a circle and have paper hats to pass round (one fewer than the number of children). When the music stops all those with a hat put them on their heads. The player with no hat drops out, taking a hat with him. The game then carries on until there is only one player left, who is the winner.

THE CAKE

Menu 1
Plenty of possibilities! Stripes, marbling, zig zags; anything red and green. I've gone for the splatter look.

Menu 2
Well – it has to be an upside down cake!

pulling funny faces, making silly noises – anything except touching the other team. When anyone is made to laugh they are out. When the whole of one team is out it is their turn to make the others laugh, and as a finale the two who had straight faces the longest can face each other alone and try to make each other laugh.

THE ANKLE GAME
Divide the players into two teams. Send one team out of the room and ask the others to lie down on the floor in a straight row, having first taken off their shoes and socks. Drape a sheet over them so that only their feet and ankles are showing, and put numbers next to them on scraps of paper on the floor (or you could put sticky labels on their feet, which would cause extra merriment!) They must then keep completely quiet while the other team is brought in. The members of the other team must inspect the feet and ankles and make a list of which belong

The red and green drinks, LEFT TO RIGHT: raspberry milkshake, mint milkshake, lemonade with grenadine, lemonade with peppermint. This is not the party to worry about food colourings – add a little if necessary.

The topsy-turvy meal: everything inside out or upside down – but how did I get the drinks to stay in the glasses? (see below for the secret . . .)

Menu 1	**Menu 2**
Red and Green	*Topsy Turvy*
Red and green vegetables (peppers, carrots, celery, radishes, spring onions, etc.)	Raspberry jelly served in upside down wineglass
Tomato and avocado dips	Back to front hamburgers (i.e. burgers on the outside, half bun in the centre)
Wholemeal sandwiches	Chips *on* the ketchup
Red and green iced biscuits	Lettuce *on top of* the tomato
Red and green jelly	
Little red and green cakes	
Red and green drinks	

AGE 9

When my daughter was nine, she decided she was far too grown-up to have a party and that she would just like to go to the cinema with a few friends. How wonderfully easy I thought! A few phone calls to invite them, a nearby cinema where I could relax with them in comfort, and then a quick pizza or fish and chips on the way home . . . A few days before the great day she changed her mind . . . Yes, I know I should have made her keep to her original choice but if you can't indulge them on their birthday – after all they'll be adults before we know it.

I decorated the space age table with bubble-pack over silver foil.
You can buy the beautiful silver sweets from good confectioners.

TIME AND PLACE

You may not need to have the larger parties of the six to eight age groups so it's possible you can return to using home again if you've been having to hire outside space. Either lunch or a late tea is the best time to have it, or a sleep over would probably still be good fun.

NUMBERS

Not necessarily the whole class – perhaps just ten or so.

THEMES

It's likely the birthday person will feel he/she is a bit beyond dressing up parties, but you could do something very modern like:

Space
The guests needn't dress up unless they want to, but you could make the room look very space age with lots of silver foil and plastics.

ENTERTAINMENT

As they arrive
MAKING THEIR OWN PIZZAS
Have ready a line of pizza bases (either home-made or bought) and a selection of toppings, such as tomato sauce, mushrooms, mozzarella cheese, olives, peperoni, ham, herbs, anchovies etc, in little bowls. Each guest is invited to assemble their own pizza, which will be cooked later for the meal.

Before and after the meal
ORANGES UNDER CHIN
Divide the players into two teams and stand them in two lines. The first player in each line is given an orange, which must be passed down the line *under the chin* and without being touched at all by anyone's hands. The team to pass their orange right along the line wins.

KIM'S GAME
Put a selection of twenty or so objects on a tray. Give every child a pencil and paper and sit them in a circle. Place the tray in the middle of the

Making their own pizzas from a delicious selection of toppings.

circle and tell the children they have thirty seconds to study what is on the tray – they must not write anything yet. Remove the tray and tell them to write down as many things as they can remember; allow about three minutes for this, depending on their writing skill. The player who has correctly listed the most objects is the winner.

CONSEQUENCES
Give each child a piece of paper. They are going to write something at the top of the paper (without their neighbour seeing), then fold over the paper where they have just written and pass the paper to the player on their left. Then more will be written, another fold made and the paper passed on again. At the end, the papers are opened out and the short stories read out.

This is what they have to write:
1   An adjective describing a person (e.g. silly).
2   The name of a girl (e.g. Snow White).
3   The word 'met', and an adjective that describes a person (e.g. tiny).
4   The name of a boy or man (e.g. Batman).
5   The word 'at' and the name of a place (e.g. Windsor Castle).
6   The words 'he said to her' and what he said (e.g. 'Two coca-colas please').

7 The words 'she said to him' and what she said (e.g. 'If you do I'll call the police').

8 The words 'And the consequence was' and what it was (e.g. 'They lived happily ever after').

If this story was read out at the end of the game it would sound like this: 'Silly Snow White met tiny Batman at Windsor Castle. He said to her 'Two coca-colas please'. She said to him 'If you do I'll call the police'. And the consequence was they lived happily ever after.' All the stories will be very funny, especially if players starts to include the names of teachers . . . and the giggles will build up if you play several rounds.

SPOT THE SQUEEZE

All the players but one stand in a circle with their hands by their sides. The remaining player stands in the middle. On the word 'GO!' one of the players in the circle squeezes the hand of the player next to him. That player has to pass the squeeze on round the circle – the squeeze can go in any direction, clockwise one moment, anti-clockwise the next. The player in the middle has to spot the squeeze, and when he catches someone squeezing their neighbour's hand the caught squeezer moves into the middle and the player in the middle joins the circle.

ZOO TIME

Hide buttons all over the place (or you could use green pennies, see page 42). Pair off all the players, and tell each couple what animals they are. Send one of each pair off to search for buttons. Everytime someone finds a button, he must make his animal noise – a bark, a moo etc, and his partner on hearing the noise must go to find him. The partner takes the button while the looker goes off again to look for more. The partner must never follow, but must wait to hear the correct animal noise before setting out to join him to take the most recent button. Fix a time limit – say five minutes – and the couple with the most buttons at the end wins. Then reverse the lookers and waiters and start again.

HOT CHOCOLATE

All the players sit cross legged at one end of the room throwing a dice. When a player throws a six, he gets up and rushes to a bar of chocolate on a plate at the other end of the room. He has to try to eat the chocolate *with a knife and fork*. He must not touch it with his hands at all. The others meanwhile have continued throwing the dice, and as soon as anyone throws a six he runs to take over the chocolate eating. You may need several bars of chocolate for this popular game!

DOLL DRESSING

Divide the players into pairs. Each pair is given a doll and some clothes in which to dress it. The first pair to dress their doll wins – but *they can only use one hand each.*

WHAT'S THE SMELL?

Lay out six saucers on a tray and fill them with something that has a strong, recognisable smell – cocoa, curry powder, a rose, orange peel, or coffee for example. Don't let the players see the tray. Blindfold all the players and let them take it in turns to sniff the saucers. They mustn't touch. When everyone had had a sniff, remove the tray and ask them to write down what they thought was in the saucers.

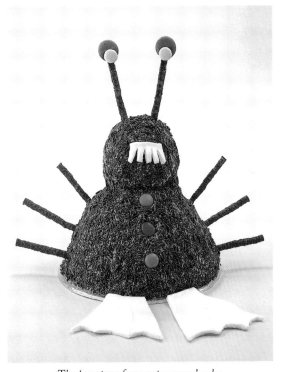

The 'creature from outer space' cake.

Playing the fashion game. LEFT: *Annabel and B being dressed up.* RIGHT: *Eleanor and Jenny get the treatment.* BELOW: *It's fun to be able to give them all instant photographs to take home.*

FASHION PARADE

Provide heaps of old clothes, egg boxes, safety pins, bits of material and pieces of paper, string, staplers, sellotape, hats, feathers – almost anything you can lay your hands on. Divide the players into pairs. One from each pair must dress up the other in as fantastic a way as he/she likes. Set a time limit, of say ten minutes, and then one by one the 'models' must parade their outfits while their dressers describe them to the audience. Then let the pairs swap and the models take a turn at being the designers. If you can take photographs or video of everyone so much the better.

THE CAKE

Anything to do with space. I've chosen a Transformer and a Creature from Outer Space.

Menu

Uncooked pizza bases with bowls of colourful toppings (e.g. sweetcorn, pepper, mushrooms, tomatoes, ham, anchovies, tuna, egg, etc)

Salads

Chocolate brownies

Into double figures! Make them feel really sophisticated with a disco party or an evening outing. Clothes needn't be expensive – at the back of the book is the design for our simple disco skirt.

The magnificent disco cake. You could stick sparklers into any kind of cake or pudding to make it celebratory, but do watch out for safety.

TIME AND PLACE

It might be exciting to give the party more towards the evening time. As long as it's a weekend or in the holidays most parents won't mind if the children are up a little later than usual. Home is probably the best place to give it, or a hired restaurant – but that could be expensive.

NUMBERS

Entirely dependent on how the birthday person is feeling.

THEME

A disco party could go down very well – either for all girls or for mixed. Hire a really good disco and try to leave them alone for a bit.

The disco: let the guests take turns at being the DJ – they'll love it.

ENTERTAINMENT

If you are having a disco ask the organiser if he is planning any games. If not, try to plan some dancing competitions and musical games and discuss with him when and how to arrange them. Some of the following might also be enjoyed at this age:

ONE MINUTE WALK

The aim of this game is to get the players to cross the room in *exactly one minute*. Line them all up at one end, confiscate their watches, cover up the clocks, and on the word 'GO!' let them start walking. They must take even paces, but can move as slowly as they like. Anyone who stops midway, or reaches the other side too soon is out. The player nearest the other side when the minute is up has won.

BALLOON BLOW

Form teams, with no more than three players in each team and give each team a balloon. On the word 'GO!' the balloons must be thrown up in the air and kept afloat by their teams *blowing* at them. No balloon must be touched by heads, hands or shoulders. The team that keeps its balloon longest in the air, wins.

BLIND MAN'S TREASURE HUNT

Wrap enough parcels so there is one for every player. Send everyone out of the room and place the parcels on the floor. Bring the players back, one by one and blindfolded and let them choose a parcel. When everyone has chosen they can take off their blindfolds and unwrap their parcels. This is where the fun comes in, because in all the smaller parcels you will have wrapped something rather nice, like a sweet or a brooch, and in all the large parcels something very odd, like a potato or a piece of coal!

A-TISSUE

Divide the players into two teams, who must then sit in two circles. Each player must have a straw ready in his mouth. Give each team a piece of tissue paper, which must be passed round the team by sucking it on to a straw and then blowing out gently as it is passed on to the next team member. Only if it is dropped may it be touched – just to pick it up and return it to the straw. The first team to pass it right round wins.

RHYMING DUMBSHOW

Divide the players into two teams. One team leaves the room while the other chooses a *verb* – sing, dance, play, walk, run or jump for example. The other team now returns and is told a word that *rhymes* with the one they have to guess. For example, if the chosen verb were 'hop' they would be told that the secret verb rhymes with 'stop'. The team trying to guess the word now has to act out the word they think it is in dumb show. If they begin to flop about the other team hisses, because the verb isn't 'flop'. They hiss at every wrong guess until the acting team start to hop about, when the other team cheers. Teams take it in turns to be the choosers or the guessers.

THE CAKE

An ice cream cake will cool down the disco-dancers but I've added sparklers to make it really festive (page 91). If you decide to serve our ice cream sundaes (below) you could make the cake of sponge only.

Smoky bacon drumsticks.

Let the guests assemble their own ice cream sundaes.

Menu

Smoky bacon drumsticks

Salad

Bowls of differently flavoured ice creams
(e.g. vanilla, blackcurrant, raspberry,
strawberry, chocolate, mint)

Toppings for ice cream (e.g. flaked almonds,
mixed nuts, sliced peaches, bananas, apricots,
fresh raspberries, strawberries, hundreds and
thousands, various sauces, etc)

AGE 11

The penultimate of our parties, and for children well into their individual likes and dislikes. You will have to listen carefully to the birthday person's instructions, as there's probably some popular way of doing things that is absolutely essential if the party isn't going to be uncool . . .

Chloë, Paul and Daisy wearing the T-shirts they decorated. The fairground flags in the background are made from paper napkins draped over lengths of string.

TIME, PLACE AND NUMBERS

Just as for age 10. You might consider getting together with a group of other parents and doing something really dramatic, like hiring a funfair or a battleship! (See page 127).

THEME

But if that's out of the question, how about making your home into a miniature funfair? No, I'm not suggesting dodgems around the sitting room – just a few side stalls and some flags around the place.

ENTERTAINMENT

As they arrive

Buy a cheap white T-shirt for every child. Spread out plenty of beads, ribbons, fabric markers, badges, needles and threads, embroidery wools, paste jewels and so on, for them to decorate their own T-shirts.

Red and white check paper or plastic cloths over tea chests make good 'stalls'.

Decorating the T-shirts.

Before and after the meal
Good games to set up on stalls:

BUCKET BALL

Stand the players behind a line about 6½ feet (2 metres) from a bucket and get them to throw a ping-pong ball into the bucket. Usually the ball will bounce out, but every time it stays there the player gets a point. Everyone gets ten throws and the player with the highest score wins.

HANGING OUT THE WASHING

String a clothes line across a corner of the room. Have a basket ready full of clothes pegs, and on the word 'GO!' the player has to clip as many clothes pegs as he can on to the line in thirty seconds. The player with the highest score at the end wins.

THIMBLES ON NAILS

See page 52.

SMARTIES ON STRAWS

See page 52.

FEEL IT

Hide a selection of small objects in a pillow case. Each player must come and feel the pillow case and write down his name and what he thinks is inside the pillow case on a piece of paper. Keep the papers until the end and then see who has the most right. Good objects to hide are apples, oranges, toothbrushes, whistles, combs, egg cups, corkscrews, coins, thimbles, pencils, keys, matchsticks, toys and so on.

Other games
BANG BANG RACE

Divide the players into two teams. They must sit on chairs in two rows facing each other about

The fairground cake. The balls are some extraordinary gobstoppers which my mother found in her local newsagent.

6½ feet (2 metres) apart. Under each chair is a paper bag. On the word 'GO!' the first player in each team gets up, races between all the chairs on her side, down the pathway between the two teams and back to her own chair. As soon as she sits down, she must pick up her paper bag, blow it up and burst it by hitting it with her hand. The bursting of the bag is the signal for the second player to set out round the chairs and back to his own where he blows up his bag and bursts it, and so on down the line. The first team to have burst all its bags has won.

THIMBLE RACE

Into two teams again. The teams stand in line, each member holding a straw in her mouth. The leader of each team is given a thimble which she places on the end of her straw. She then has to turn to the next player in line and pass the thimble on to that player's straw. That player then turns to the next player and passes the thimble on to her in exactly the same way. The first team to have sent the thimble all the way from one end to the other has won. If the thimble is dropped (and it will be!) it must be returned to the leader who places it on the end of her straw to start all over again.

BLINDFOLD OBSTACLE RACE

Send all the players out of the room. Bring one pair back in, whose inside legs must then be tied together, just like a three legged race. While they are watching, prepare an obstacle course; make it look really difficult, with chairs upturned, cushions everywhere and nasty things to bump into. Blindfold them and turn them round and round a few times so they don't really know which way they are facing. While you are doing this, have your accomplices silently remove all the obstacles. Then tell the pair you are going to time them round the course, give them the word 'GO!' and watch them trying to race round the course avoiding obstacles that aren't even there! Once they have finished they can take their blindfolds off and then watch the next pair going through the same silly routine – but don't let them give anything away. Nobody wins this race, but everyone should have plenty of laughs!

IN THE MANNER OF THE WORD

One player leaves the room, while the other players choose an 'acting' word, such as angrily, happily, hurriedly etc. When the player who was sent out comes back, he has to guess the word. To help him, he can ask any of the others to perform a certain task *in the manner of the word*. He can ask them to untie their shoe laces, open a window or read from a book and they must do it in the way described by the word – angrily, happily and so on. As soon as the player has guessed the word someone else leaves the room and another word is chosen.

POOR PUSSY

A very silly game that isn't nearly as easy as it sounds. Divide the players into two equal rows and get them to face each other about 6 feet (2 metres) apart. The first player must go to the player opposite him, kneel down and say 'meow!' three times. The other player must stroke the pussy who is kneeling at his feet and say 'Poor pussy!' without smiling, smirking, giggling or laughing. If he is successful he goes over to the next player in the line opposite, kneels at his

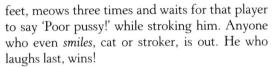

ABOVE: *Fortune cookies. No doubt you can get plenty of help in thinking up witty captions . . .* LEFT: *The spud stall. Put out a good selection and let the guests help themselves.*

feet, meows three times and waits for that player to say 'Poor pussy!' while stroking him. Anyone who even *smiles*, cat or stroker, is out. He who laughs last, wins!

THE CAKE

I've made a Roll-a-ball cake (page 91), but anything to do with the fair would do.

Menu

Baked potatoes with bowls of topping (e.g. tuna in mayonnaise, thousand island dressing, blue cheese, tomato relish, shrimp in yoghurt, soured cream and chives)

Toffee apples

Fortune cookies

AGE 12

The last of our birthday parties — but probably not the last for you — soon it'll be time for the teenage parties and all the problems and joys they will bring. Enjoy these children's parties while they last and give the birthday person the treat of feeling really grown-up and sophisticated while you still think of him/her as your baby . . .

LEFT TO RIGHT: Chelsee, Jimmy, Ben, Vivene, Kolya and Daisy look very elegant in their evening clothes, sipping their grape juice. There were lots of giggles at first — they'd never seen each other looking so smart — but all agreed it was a very special party.

TIME, PLACE AND NUMBERS

Late afternoon or early evening is probably the best time, although in summer an outdoor lunch party or barbecue would be wonderful. This might well be the time to take a small group to the cinema or theatre, or perhaps to a local restaurant. A good Chinese meal can be great fun at this age, or of course Italian food is always much appreciated – take-away pizzas can be ordered by telephone and collected just before meal time. Borrow a menu from the pizza restaurant and let the children choose which one they would like to eat.

THEME

Make it as near to an adult evening as you can, but without losing the charm of it being for twelve-year-olds. Start them off with a choice of intriguing 'cocktails', followed by an elegant dinner party. Or have just a 'cocktail' party, by inviting larger numbers and serving them a good variety of 'finger food'.

ENTERTAINMENT

A professional entertainer will probably not be very popular unless it's a sophisticated magician or illusionist. But the children will still enjoy well-organised games.

As they arrive

Use your 'cocktail bar' as the perfect ice-breaker. At my daughter's twelfth birthday I made a menu of non-alcoholic cocktails and called them after some of the children's schoolteachers and after the children themselves: 'Sarah's passion', 'A Mrs Howe Special' etc. It was a huge success and after a couple of rounds the girls started inventing their own mixtures.

Various fruit juices, fizzy drinks and syrups made into 'cocktails'.

WHO AM I?

As they arrive, each guest has a slip of paper pinned to his/her back, with the name of a famous person – fact or fiction – written on it. They have to find out who they are, by asking other guests questions about themselves, but only questions calling for a 'Yes' or 'No' answer. If you choose some silly names like 'Sooty', 'Father Christmas' or 'Donald Duck' as well as some more serious historical ones, the game can be great fun, and will help the guests get to know each other.

Before and after the meal

CHARADES AND WRITTEN GAMES would go down well (pages 56 and 52).

WHAT ARE WE SHOUTING?

Players divide into two teams and the first team goes away into a corner and thinks of a well-known phrase or proverb. Let's suppose it is 'A stitch in time saves nine'. If there are six members of the team, each member is given a different word to shout. If there are more than six, then some members will have to shout the same word. When they have chosen the phrase and sorted out who is going to shout which word, they go over to the other team and on the word 'GO!' they shout all their words together. The other team can ask to hear the words shouted three times before it must guess what the phrase

is. If they get it wrong, the shouting team chooses another phrase and shouts it again. When it is guessed, the teams change places. Some good phrases to shout are:
God save the Queen (for four players).
Hark the herald angels sing (for five players).
Too many cooks spoil the broth (for six players).
Little Jack Horner sat in a corner (for seven players).

Naughty Letter

A very difficult game. Tell all the players that one particular letter in the alphabet is banned, and tell them that letter. Then ask the players questions, one by one. They must answer straight away, but if the answer contains the banned letter, they are out!

The Vicar's Cat

The players sit in a circle and one of them is chosen to begin. He starts by saying: 'The vicar's cat is an *attractive cat* and her name is *Ann.*' He can say whatever he likes, as long as the adjective and the name begin with 'A'. The next player has to offer a similar sentence, but with the adjective and name beginning with 'B', and so on round the circle, using every letter of the alphabet except 'X'. Each player has five seconds to think of his sentence, and if he goes over that time he is out. If there is still more than one player left when you have been right through the alphabet, then start at 'A' all over again, but only using adjectives and names that were *not* used in the first round.

Blindfold Drawing

Get all the players to sit round a table with paper and pencil to hand. Now blindfold them. Now tell them to draw a house. When they have finished drawing their houses, and just as they think the game is over, tell them to draw a garden in front of the house. Then tell them to draw some hills behind the house. Then tell them to add clouds to the sky. Then tell them to draw curtains at the windows. Finally tell them

to put a policeman in the garden. When everyone has finished, take off the blindfolds and give a prize to the person who has drawn the most accurate – or the craziest! – picture. My father always said this game was a good test of cheating – if any picture is very accurate you might be justified in feeling suspicious . . .

Drawing Clumps

Divide the players into two teams. Before the party, write down twice on separate pieces of paper objects that must be guessed by the teams. You need at least enough for each team member to have one turn. You can make them quite difficult: 'The last stitch in the Queen's coronation robes', 'The tallest man in Africa', 'The most poisonous plant in Battersea park' and so on. Fold the clues over and number them on the outside in opposite order, so the teams will not be guessing the same clues at the same time. Write the numbers clearly in different colours for each team. On the word 'GO!' one member of each team must rush to collect their no. 1 clue (in our house we put the clues on a different floor, so there's plenty of frantic rushing up and down stairs!) They must return to their teams (who are out of earshot of each other) and then as quickly as possible *draw* the clue for their own team to guess. The drawer can only answer yes or no, but the team members must fire all sorts of questions as they watch the drawing. This does *not* depend on being a good artist, but on drawing non-stop and approaching the subject from different angles when the team gets stuck. An adult must supervise each team to see that there is no cheating and that the phrase is guessed completely accurately. When it is, another team member dashes to the next clue, and so on.

THE CAKE

This combines with the fruit salad to make the pudding. (Yes, I know we've got grapes in both courses, but at least they're a different colour!)

The elegant dinner: smoked salmon pâté, chicken with grapes, chocolate mousse and the 'cake'.

Menu 1	**Menu 2**
Cocktail Party	*Dinner Party*
Chive biscuits, avocado dip	Smoked salmon pâté
Baby sausages with barbecue dip	Chicken with grapes
Bacon rolls	Exotic fruit salad
Smoked salmon canapés	Chocolate mousse
Mini pizza	
Pineapple cheese and cherry sticks	
Prawn tartlets	
Stuffed cherry tomatoes with cream cheese and basil	

HALLOWE'EN

It has become a tradition in our house to have a Hallowe'en party every year for the children. It's certainly a marvellous excuse to put on some spooky costumes and play a few games, and as I don't like the idea of firework parties for young children unless they're professionally organised, a Hallowe'en party can make a good substitute.

Even the sweetest children can be little devils at times, and here's a costume to suit the part. With his wicked smile Jack looks as if he has some plans for mischief making ahead. His devil cloak and waistcoat reverse to become Dracula (see opposite).

Dominic, Jack, Jesse, Kimberley and Imogen as ghost,
Dracula, skeleton and witches.

TIME, PLACE AND NUMBERS

It will obviously depend largely on the age of the children as to what time you give the party; it should be either afternoon or evening if possible, and the later the better. For older children of say ten upwards, let the party go on until 8.00 or 9.00 so that they can feel the ghosts beginning to stir at the approach of midnight! It's best to give the party at home if you possibly can, and don't invite too many children or it will be hard to keep the party under control and play some of the games I've given here. I suggest twelve to fifteen at the most, and fewer if the children are young.

THEME

Buy some black crepe paper and cut out some bats, witches and so on. You could make a long string of them by folding the paper fanwise and cutting the shape before unfolding it. Buy some pumpkins well

ahead of time, as greengrocers tend to run out; scoop them out, cut them into Jack-o-Lanterns and put a candle in each one. Cover the table with black paper and make everything as spooky as possible. My father used to bring back a skeleton from the hospital where he worked and sit it at the head of the table – one year he even wired it for sound and it spoke to us! You don't have to go quite that far, but an extra guest of some sort at the table can be fun.

ENTERTAINMENT

As they arrive
DECORATING HATS

Just as for decorating crowns (page 51), but give them three-quarter circle shapes of black card which will be stapled into witches' hats before they leave.

Before and after the meal
BOBBING APPLES

A very wet game indeed, but a classic for Hallowe'en. Spread out plenty of newspaper – or better still a plastic cloth – on the floor and place on it a very large bowl full of water. Have a large bib or apron ready for each player. Float some apples in the water, and then one by one the

BELOW RIGHT: Dracula's cloak, waistcoat, gloves and teeth!
LEFT: Reversed plus horns and tail to be a devil.

players must kneel down and with their arms behind their backs, try to lift an apple out of the water. For young children you could leave on the stalks, which makes it much easier.

BUNS ON STRINGS
Thread a fruit bun for each child on to a length of string, then tie the strings on to another piece of string which you fasten like a washing line across the room. Try to get the height of each bun in a suitable place for a child to reach it with their mouth. With their hands behind their backs, the children must try to eat their buns – the first to finish is the winner.

WITCH HUNT
This game can be scary, so it is not suitable if the children are very young. A witch is chosen, and sent to hide somewhere in the house. As soon as the witch has had time to hide, all the lights are turned out and the witch-hunters set out to find the witch. If the hunters call out 'Where are you, witch?' the witch, who can move about as much as she likes (or dares) in the dark, has to answer with a witch-like cackle. Whoever catches the witch becomes the witch for the next round.

DUSTY MILLER
Get out the plastic cloth and the bibs again! This is a marvellous, messy game. In the middle of the cloth – or large sheet – place a bowl half filled with flour. Mixed up with the flour are six well scrubbed twopenny pieces. The players have to kneel by the bowl, their arms folded behind their backs, and fish out as many coins as they can, using only their teeth. Some players will bury their faces in flour – the clever ones will simply *blow* at the flour until a coin is unearthed, when they will pick it up with their teeth.

Whichever method is used, a good time will be had by all.

SARDINES
See page 43.

MUSICAL TORCH
This goes down very well with children who love to frighten one another. The players sit on the floor in a circle and all the lights are turned out. One player is given a lighted torch and when the music plays the torch is passed from hand to hand around the group. Whoever is holding the torch when the music stops is out. To make the game as eerie as possible each player should hold the torch just below the chin and while the music is playing make all sorts of ghostly noises.

THE WITCH'S STORY
An essential part of our Hallowe'en. While the children are out of the room, prepare a tray of items that could *feel* like parts of the human body – peeled grapes for eyes, wet flannel for skin, raw sausage for finger, cooked spaghetti for veins and arteries, warm milk for blood, etc. An adult then dresses as a witch (just a dark blanket draped over will do, as it will be too dark to see much anyway) and invites the children into a dark room to hear her story. They must sit in a circle in front of her (or him) and the witch will tell how she likes to eat juicy little children and how she has been lucky enough to catch one today. Would the children like to feel some of the bits she is going to have for her dinner? Then she passes the nasty-feeling items around the circle, describing them as they go round and letting each child feel them. You must obviously suit the 'spookiness' of your voice and story to the age of the children, but it's usually a very popular game with all ages.

THE CAKE

I've made little Hallowe'en spiders but there are other possibilities (page 92).

Hallowe'en spider cakes, severed hand sandwich, filled pitta bread faces, spooky black biscuits. Cut shapes out of a black paper cloth and put it over a yellow or orange one. Add scooped-out pumpkins and plastic skeletons.

Menu

Filled pitta bread faces
Spooky black biscuits
Severed hand sandwiches

 EASTER

The spring can be a lovely time of year to give a children's party. If your children's birthdays are in the winter (my two sons' are) it's a good excuse to have a small celebration to break up the long wait for the next birthday party.

Yellow crepe paper and plastic flowers stapled onto an old gardening hat.

Ears cut from fake fur stapled onto a plastic party fez.

Part of an old feather boa, plus a ping pong ball and red felt trimming, glued to a straw hat.

A fur egg cosy and some gold lace, plus some egg shells and ribbon all glued onto a felt trilby.

Napkin glued over a paper bowl, blown egg glued onto plastic egg-cup (plus plastic spoon) glued onto napkin. Add elastic.

Yellow and green crepe paper, florist's wire and a smart straw hat I found at a jumble sale.

TIME, PLACE AND NUMBERS

Try to hold the party as near to Easter Day as possible. Tea-time is the traditional time for it, and the length will depend on the ages of the children you are inviting (see Birthday Parties for ideas of timing for different ages). If the weather looks as if it is going to be good then it would be lovely to hold the party in a garden or park, and if you do then invite plenty of children – once you're out of doors it's much easier to cope with large numbers.

THEME

Send egg-shaped invitations. Cover the table with white and yellow crepe paper and decorate it with cut-out chicks, eggs and real or fake daffodils. You could put a chocolate egg at each place setting, covered with a little home-made egg cosy which the child can take home at the end.

Decorating eggs can be great fun. Hard boil them first (or blow them if they are to keep).

ENTERTAINMENT

As they arrive

EGG HUNT

Before the party, hide lots of little chocolate Easter eggs all over the house (or garden, better still). As each child arrives, give her a basket or bag and set her off to search for as many eggs as she can find. It might be wise to keep some eggs back that you can surreptitiously hide as late-comers arrive, or for those who are bad lookers.

Before and after the meal

Depending on the age group of the guests, choose some of the party games given in the Birthday Parties. If the party is in the park or garden, use some of the games given for Outdoor Parties (page 86). The following may also be especially suitable:

EGG THROWING

No, you don't throw real eggs – the aim of the game is to bounce a ping pong ball into an empty egg carton from a distance of about 6½ feet (2 metres). Each player has three goes and the player who manages to land the ball in

the carton most often, wins. If you like, you can number the compartments in the egg carton, so that bouncing a ball into one compartment scores more than bouncing it into another. If you play the game this way, the player with the highest score wins.

PASS THE BALL

Divide the players into two equal teams and seat them on the floor facing each other, with legs outstretched but not touching. A ball is now placed on the ankles of the players at the head of each team and the aim of the game is to pass the ball from player to player using ankles only. If the ball touches the floor, it must be passed back to the first player who has to start all over again. The first team that manages to pass its ball from one end to the other without dropping it wins.

SPOON EGGS

The players divide into two teams and each team forms a line. Each player holds a spoon in his/her mouth. The aim of the race is to pass a chocolate egg (do find hollow, light ones!) from spoon to spoon down the line. No hands at all

The Easter bunny cake is very simple to make.

are allowed – if the egg is dropped it must be picked up by the spoon still held in the mouth.

EGG GUESSING
Find a cardboard Easter egg and fill it with a carefully counted selection of small sweets. The egg is passed around the group of children, who are sitting on the floor. They may feel the weight of the egg and shake it gently, and all must try to guess how many sweets are inside. The one who comes nearest to the correct total wins the sweets.

THE CAKE

This cuddly Easter bunny makes a change from chickens or Simnel cakes.

The Humpty Eggs make a perfect Easter meal.

Menu

Choose some food from our Birthday Parties.
The Humpty Eggs (page 35) would be very
suitable.

CHRISTMAS

What a special time to give a party – to celebrate the most wonderful birthday of them all. Whatever your religion – or lack of it – no one can fail to be moved by the spirit of Christmas, especially when it comes to anything to do with children. The sight of little children looking like angels while they hold their candles and sing carols in church reduces me to a hopeless jelly of emotion, even when I know they'll be at each other's throats ten minutes later . . .

Christmas biscuits (you can buy suitable cutters at most good stores) and the igloo cake. I've used transparent snowflake wrapping paper over a red tablecloth.

TIME, PLACE AND NUMBERS

Try to have the party near to Christmas, but remember that some families go away for the festivities, so be sure to check that enough friends will be around before you set the date. Don't invite too many children unless you have plenty of help, as there will be quite enough work to do preparing for Christmas without giving yourself too much extra. Either a lunchtime or teatime party would be suitable.

THEME

It would of course be best to have the Christmas decorations up before the party so that your setting is truly Christmassy. Hang some little presents on the tree that the children can take home – perhaps chocolate figures or coins, or tiny parcels with rubbers, sweets or badges inside. Don't forget Christmas crackers on the table – they add enormously to the fun.

ENTERTAINMENT

According to the age of your guests, pick some of the games from the Birthday Party section. Some of the following may be especially appreciated.

As they arrive
Decorating Trees

Have ready a Christmas tree shape cut out of green card for each child. Spread out plenty of glue, glitter, sequins, stickers, little sticky stars, bits of tinsel and so on, for the children to decorate their trees. When they are finished write their names on the back, stick a loop on top of each and give to the children when they go home.

Before and after the meal
Christmas Stocking Story

This is an excellent game for children of about four upwards; it needs a grown-up who is good at telling stories. Sit the players on the ground

LEFT TO RIGHT: *Holly headdress, easy Father Christmas, Christmas tree and a snowman.*

and give them their 'parts'. One of them will be given a name, the others must all be toys that might be put into a child's stocking – teddy bear, train, doll and so on. When they all know what they are, the story begins. Every time the child who has been given a name is mentioned, he or she must get up, turn around and then sit down again. Every time one of the toys is mentioned that player must get up and turn round in the same way. And every time the word 'stocking' is mentioned, *all* the players must get up and turn around before sitting down again.

MERRY CHRISTMAS

A game for slightly older children – say seven upwards. The players form a circle. One player starts the game by counting 'One'. The player to the left follows with 'Two', and so on round the group, except that whenever the number five or any of its multiples comes up, the player whose turn it is must say 'Merry Christmas' instead of the number. Any player who forgets to say 'Merry Christmas', or says it in the wrong place or who says something like 'Happy Christmas' instead, is out.

CHRISTMAS CARD HUNT

Exactly as for matching postcards (page 38) but use old Christmas cards (so remember to keep them this year in case you want to play this next year!) You could put all the halves in a large basket and let the players match up as many as they can in a given time. Hide the other halves in easy or difficult places according to the age group playing.

VISITING FATHER CHRISTMAS

This can be a really exciting adventure. Find an adult to dress up as Father Christmas and put him if possible in a room by himself. Make the room as cave-like and intriguing as possible – put a red bulb in the light for instance, and drape the walls with paper or sheets. Construct a 'tunnel' leading to the cave, by bending a mattress into an arch, upturning a large armchair, sticking large open cardboard boxes together or by whatever other means you can devise. Drape the tunnel with white sheets to make it look snowy. One by one the children can crawl

The Christmas tree costume – mostly made of crepe paper.

through the tunnel to visit Father Christmas who will of course give them a little present from his sack. If it's an adult the children don't know, so much the better: it's not quite so magical if they come out saying 'It's really Charlie's Dad with cotton wool on his face . . .'

THE CAKE

Either a traditional cake, or something more unusual, like our Igloo.

Menu

Pick some festive food from our birthday selection and include some Christmassy biscuits. Some of the red and green food (page 58) would look very seasonal.

HALF BIRTHDAY

If your child has a birthday in the depths of winter and has always wanted an outdoors party, or if he/she has a birthday in the middle of the school holidays when everyone is always away, you could give a 'Half-birthday party'. It can be great fun and a good excuse to have a party in a long stretch of the year when not much else is happening.

Some food for a half birthday – if you're feeling extravagant why not cut the table in half too . . .

TIME, PLACE AND NUMBERS

Plan the party for about the time when your child's half-birthday will fall. Depending on the age, choose a suitable number of children and time of day (see Birthday Parties), but plan to start and finish the party on the half-hour. For example rather than the usual 3.00 to 5.00, make it 3.30 to 5.30.

THEME

Send out half invitations – make sure you still include all the necessary information, but write in on *half* an invitation. Make it clear that the party is to celebrate the important event of Johnny or Susie becoming eight *and a half*, or whatever age it is. You could if you like ask the guests to come half-dressed in some way, and make the party room follow your half theme in some way. You could cover up half the clock, lay half the table and so on.

ENTERTAINMENT

As they arrive
MATCHING POSTCARDS
See page 38.

Before and after the meal
FIND THE OTHER HALF
Have ready a pair of shoes and socks for each child. Some adult shoes and socks would be ideal, and if you can include some strange ones like flippers, climbing boots or wellingtons, so much the better. The children must take off their own shoes and socks and stand behind a starting line. They are given one sock and shoe each, and on the word 'GO!' they must put them on, then run to a box which is filled with the remaining socks. They must find their matching socks, put them on, then run back to the starting line. From there they run to another box which is full of the remaining shoes. They find their matching shoes then run back to the starting line to win the game. Put the boxes as far apart as you can – you could even have them in different rooms.

For the rest of the party, look through Birth-

Two half-dressed guests admiring the half-cake.

days 1 to 12 for more game ideas. If you want to show a film or video, what about 'Half a Sixpence'!

THE CAKE

Half a cake, naturally.

Menu

Serve whatever food you like, but make sure you cut everything (including the paper plates) in half!

OUTDOOR

My birthday is in April, and on a couple of occasions my parents gave me birthday parties in the park – I still remember what fun they were. It's difficult to predict the weather – but as long as you have some contingency plan for the dash to cover in the event of rain, an out of doors party can be one of the best of all.

The beehive cake and a little plastic bucket filled with a transportable tea.

TIME, PLACE AND NUMBERS

Unless you're thinking of bonfire night or Hallowe'en you've obviously got to have the party in the daytime; lunchtime might be the best, as it'll allow plenty of playing time after the meal without danger of late afternoon chilliness setting in. If you'd rather have it at tea-time then make it as early as you can.

If you're lucky enough to have a large garden – or a friend with a field – then you don't need to think any further. The alternatives for those of us with small paved patios are to use a nearby park, school playing field or local recreation ground. Invite as many children as you can – it's far easier to have large numbers when you're not confined in a small room, and races need to have enough competitors to make them exciting.

THEME

If you're giving it in your own garden it could be fun to have a Tarzan party by making your garden as jungly as you can – perhaps draping a draught-stopper snake in one of the trees and so on – but it's not worth too much effort. The delight of being able to run around and let off steam in the open air is theme enough of its own. Of course if you want to disguise all the trees as chessmen or dress the local cats as Martians it's up to you, but don't give yourself too much work.

ENTERTAINMENT

Don't forget that most of the indoor games given in the Birthday Parties can perfectly well be played outside. Here are a few more that are particularly suitable for out of doors:

As they arrive
For young children:
GARDEN FUN
Have ready a sandpit with plenty of spades, buckets, sieves, old yoghurt cartons etc. The more toys you can find the better – swings, tricycles, play tunnels, slides and so on. If the weather is hot enough, fill the paddling pool and have plenty of towels to hand.

The cakes that look amazingly like ice creams.

For older children:
MINIATURE COLLECTIONS
Give each child a matchbox and tell him/her to collect as many things as possible *that will fit into the box*. When everyone has finished, count up and see who has collected the most.

Before and after the meal
For young children:
Little children enjoy any sort of race, but make sure you include some sitting games like pass-the-parcel as well, so that they don't get too puffed out.

EGG AND SPOON RACE
Give each child a dessertspoon with a small chocolate egg in it. Whoever crosses the finishing line with the egg still in the spoon is the winner, but as everyone wins a chocolate egg, you shouldn't have too many tears from the losers. You will have to judge from the ages involved how firm to be about cheating; running the whole race with hand firmly clasped over the egg should not be encouraged . . .

CHAIN TAG

Two players join hands and together chase the others. Whenever they touch anyone, that child joins hands with them and helps them chase the others. Gradually a chain builds up, and whoever is last to be caught is the winner.

DRESSING UP RACE

A very popular game, and good for getting giggly. Have ready lots of old clothes. On the word 'GO!' the children run from the starting line to their individual piles of clothes, put them on and run back to the start. You may have to race in heats if you haven't enough clothes for all.

SACK RACE

Use strong brown paper carrier bags (or plastic ones, but do make sure they are all collected up safely after the race). Each child is given a 'sack' and stands at the starting line. On the word 'GO' the children must race to the finishing line, by hopping in their bags, while holding the handles.

For older children:

DRESSING UP RACE

A more sophicated version of the younger children's race. The players divide into two teams. They are to race in relay to a finishing line. On the way to the finishing line at suitably spaced intervals you have laid out a hat, shirt, trousers and boots for each team. The players must run to the clothes, put them on as they come to them then run to the finishing line, touch it and race back again *removing the clothes in reverse order as they go and leaving them in their correct places for the next player.* Each player does the same thing, and the team to finish first is the winner.

OBSTACLE COURSE

Either run this as a team relay race or get each child to compete against the clock. Make the course as like an army assault course as possible – excellent for letting off steam. Plan as many different challenges along the route as you can, things like:

> Balancing along a plank, supported on two old tyres.
> Climbing through a suspended tyre, or crawling through a play tunnel.
> Jumping a certain distance.

Another view of my favourite cakes.

> Hopping a certain distance, in or out of a sack.
> Climbing over a large object.
> Running up a rope ladder and down again.
> Stepping stones (bricks or old telephone directories).
> Putting clothes on.
> Turning somersaults.
> Doing a high jump.
> Skipping a number of skips with a skipping rope.

TORTOISE RACE

This is a very strange race – whoever comes *last* is the winner. Set up a short course of ten metres or so. On the word 'GO!' the players set off from the starting line as *slowly as possible.* They must keep moving, but travel as slowly as they can – anyone caught stopping, even for a second, is out. The last one to the finishing line wins.

EGG AND SPOON RACE

As for younger children, but use potatoes and teaspoons. You could put a big pile of potatoes and let the children run to and fro collecting as many as they can.

SACK RACE

As for younger children, but try to find proper sacks and tie them loosely at the neck.

THREE LEGGED RACE

This can cause much giggling. Divide the players into pairs and tie one player's right ankle to the other player's left ankle. Then let the pairs race down the track.

TUG OF WAR

Divide the players into two teams. Get them to stand either side of a white line and give each team one end of a long, strong rope. Make sure the centre of the rope is over the white line. On the word 'GO!' both teams must pull for all they are worth – the first team to be pulled over the white line is the loser.

Any other kind of race will be appreciated; hopping, walking backwards and so on.

THE CAKE

Something floral or our beehive or rainbow.

An alternative to the beehive – a beautiful rainbow.

Menu

Much of the food given for Birthday Parties could be transported outside, but don't give yourself too much work. Filled pitta breads, sandwiches, little pies etc are all easy to carry around. It's a lovely idea to give each child a plastic bucket with their meal in it plus a drink and a napkin, so they can carry it wherever they like.

CAKE INSTRUCTIONS

• BEEHIVE CAKE •

This cake was inspired by Mrs Pauline Hines, who wrote to me after reading my last cake book and sent me some pictures of cakes she had made, including a beehive. I thought it was a lovely idea, and I've added florist's wire and gelatine wings to make the bees 'fly' around the hive.

> *1 pudding basin cake*
> *2 quantities butter icing*
> *yellow and black food colouring*
> *2 packets marzipan*
> *leaf gelatine*
> *florist's wire*

1   Scoop an 'entrance' out of the bottom of the cake.
2   Put the cake on a turntable, if you have one. Cover the whole cake with butter icing which you have coloured yellow by mixing in a few drops of colouring.
3   Spread the icing evenly over the cake, then take a skewer or similar instrument and, starting at the top, mark circles all round the cake.
4   Mould little bees out of marzipan and paint black stripes on to them.
5   Cut wings out of the gelatine and paint veins on to them with the black.
6   Push wings gently into the bees then stick them into the cake on the ends of the wires.

Note
If it's for a birthday you could make the right number of bees for the birthday person's age.

• CROWN CAKE •

This very grand looking cake makes a marvellous centrepiece. If the room is hot, you may find the sweets start sliding off after a while (I had terrible trouble in a television studio once under the hot lights) so keep it in a cool place if possible.

> *2 × 15cm/6in round bought light fruit cakes*
> *3 packets yellow marzipan*
> *1 quantity of royal icing*
> *red food colouring*
> *clear and coloured boiled sweets/silver balls*
> *black food colouring*

1   Stick the two cakes together with jam and a circle of marzipan. Trim top to a rounded shape.
2   Roll out marzipan and cover cake. Colour half the royal icing red, then smooth over the top and sides of the cake, to about halfway down.
3   Roll and cut a strip of marzipan about half the depth of the cake. Wrap this round the bottom of the cake.
4   Roll a strip of marzipan and cut squares. Cut slashes to corners.
5   Stick shapes onto top of marzipan strip.
6   With shell nozzle pipe 'ermine' round base, then ice pearls with small plain nozzle. Stick on sweets and silver balls with icing. Paint black flecks on 'ermine'.

• CAT CAKE •

This is one of the easiest of all the cakes to do, but is very effective and children love it. If you can't find suitable triangular cakes you could cut the shapes from an extra sponge and use the left overs for a trifle, or stick them in the freezer.

> *1 readymade 20 cm/6–8 in round jam sponge*
> *2 triangular little chocolate cakes*
> *200 g/8 oz butter icing*
> *2 chocolate buttons*
> *1 yellow Smartie*
> *50 g/2 oz plain cake covering chocolate*
> *6 Matchmakers*

1   Position cakes on a 25 cm/10 in cake board.
2   Spread butter icing over top and sides of cake and mark with a fork to resemble fur.
3   Place chocolate button eyes on cake

with half a Smartie on each stuck with a little butter icing.
4   Melt chocolate and pipe round eyes, add nose, mouth and ears. Add Matchmakers for whiskers.

• CANDLE CAKE •

Our first birthday candle is a lovely symbol of the light of a young life on its way. It would also be the perfect cake for a christening or confirmation. If you find the flowers too tricky to model from icing then you could buy some little fabric ones, or even use fresh ones.

> *675 g/1½ lb sugar paste*
> *1 large swiss roll*
> *1 tbsp apricot jam*
> *1 long Matchmaker*
> *pink, green, yellow and red food colourings*
> *50 g/2 oz icing sugar*

1   Roll out half the sugar paste on a surface dusted with cornflour, to a rectangle a little longer than the swiss roll. Brush the swiss roll with jam and roll icing round.
2   Seal edges neatly. Stand swiss roll on end. Fold icing over to cover top.
3   Trim excess away from base and stand candle on a 15 cm/6 in cake board. Cut two flame shapes from trimmings. Wet and sandwich together, placing Matchmaker between. Leave to dry.
4   Divide remaining sugar paste into thirds. Colour one-third pink and one-third green.
5   Mould roses or other simple flowers from pink icing. Leave to dry on non-stick paper. Roll out green icing and cut out rose leaves. Mark veins with a knife. Leave to dry curled over a rolling pin.
6   Mix sifted icing sugar with a little water until thick and smooth. Spoon over top of candle and ease down side to resemble drips. Paint flame with yellow and red. Push into candle. Shape remaining white decoration icing into a thick rope and

place round candle base.

7 Arrange roses and leaves on rope pressing them into the soft icing.

• DINNER PARTY CAKE •

I think at 12 most children want something a little more sophisticated than pink sugar icing and candles, so I've combined pudding and celebratory cake to make an elegant centrepiece. The redcurrant jelly glaze and the touch of coconut were added by Penny, who was helping me prepare the food for the photographs. These inspired little touches made all the difference and I'm now glazing everything in sight – how about red shiny sandwiches . . .

1 quantity of sponge mix, baked in a
ring mould
redcurrant jelly to glaze
exotic fruits (we've used grapes and mango)
desiccated coconut
cream

1 Heat the redcurrant jelly until it is liquid, then paint it all over the cake.
2 Pile the halved and pipped grapes and the mango in the middle and decorate with more half grapes around the bottom.
3 Sprinkle a little coconut over the fruit and put the candles round the top.
4 You could either serve cream separately, or whip some and put it under the fruit before you pile it in.

• DISCO CAKE •

You could add sparklers to any type of cake, but this easy recipe for an ice-cream cake is very popular. You can equally well use it for a flat cake, by splitting a baking tray cake in two horizontally and sandwiching together with cream, jam and ice-cream.

1 quantity of sponge cake mixture
jar sieved fruit jam
500 ml/1 pint double cream, whipped
1 quantity of ice cream or 1 tub of bought
450 g/1 lb sugar paste
food colourings
indoor sparklers

1 Bake sponge cake in a flat baking tray.
2 When cool, cut into strips and use it to line a pudding basin.
3 Brush the inside with hot jam, then spread with whipped cream.
4 Dollop the ice-cream into the centre, then finish with another layer of strips of sponge.
5 Freeze.
6 On the day of the party, take the cake out of the freezer. Run a knife around the edge and down the sides and turn it out.
7 Roll out the sugar paste, using a little caster sugar to stop it sticking, damp it with a little water and place over the cake, taking pleats and folds as necessary.
8 Paint some bright coloured design on to the side.
9 Keep in the freezer until about half an hour before it is to be eaten when you should move it to the fridge to soften a little.

When you want to serve it, get a couple of adults to help and divide the sparklers among you. Light them all at once, just outside the party room, then stick them quickly into the cake and make the grand entrance. Do be careful – I let one fall into my hand when we were taking the photograph, and got quite a nasty burn. Make sure you put the cake down on a non-inflammable surface such as a metal tray or large china dish, and keep it well away from anyone's eyes.

• EASTER BUNNY •

There are many themes you could use for an Easter cake, but this rabbit has a certain charm and is very simple to make. I like the way the coconut gives him a furry texture.

1 pudding basin sponge cake
2 doughnuts or similar sized cakes
450 g/1 lb sugar paste
1 packet desiccated coconut
2 quantities butter icing
pink colouring
spaghetti

1 Roll out half of the mallow icing, using a little caster sugar to prevent it sticking, and cut two ear shapes. Leave them on non-stick paper for a couple of days to dry. If you haven't got time then you could make rice paper ears instead.
2 Stick the doughnuts together with some of the butter icing. Cover the doughnuts and the cake completely with butter icing, then roll the head thoroughly in coconut.
3 Pour coconut over the cake itself,

pressing it into the icing with your hands.
4 Stick the 'head' to the top of the cake with more icing. If it doesn't seem very secure, you could put a skewer (or even a clean pencil) right through, but do remember it's there when you come to eat the cake!
5 Colour the remainder of the sugar paste pink, by adding colouring drop by drop and kneading it in, then roll and cut out a ribbon and bow for bunny's neck. Stick by wetting the icing with a little water.
6 Make pink eyes and nose from left over scraps. Push a little broken spaghetti next to his nose for whiskers.
7 When the ears are dry paint them with pink colouring. Make two slits in the top of the head with a sharp knife then push the ears gently into them.

• FAIRGROUND CAKE •

There are all sorts of ideas you could use for a fairground cake – a roundabout with little icing horses would be wonderful if you had time, or even a helter skelter. I made this roll-a-ball cake without having any idea what I could use for the balls, then my mother found these amazing gob-stoppers in her local shop.

1 quantity of sponge cake mixture
1 quantity butter icing
900 g/2 lb sugar paste
brown and black food colouring
gobstoppers

1 Bake the sponge in a baking tray.
2 Scoop out carefully little dents in suitable places, then cover each dent with a little sugar paste by rolling it out and cutting circles to fit.
3 Spread the cake with butter icing, avoiding the little white dents.
4 Colour the rest of the icing sugar brown, by adding colouring drop by drop and kneading it in, then roll out and cover the top of the cake. Find the dents underneath and carefully cut away the brown icing.
5 Cover the sides with strips of icing, leaving them slightly higher than the top to make an edge.
6 Add a strip to make the trough for the balls.
7 Leave to dry a little, then paint numbers on with black colouring and place the gobstoppers in position.

● HALF CAKE ●

You could make a half of any type of cake you choose – even chopping a bought one in two if you haven't time to make one, but it does look good to have the cut side iced over.

Simply cut a cake in two, keeping the rest for trifle or to cut with a round cutter into extra little cakes. Decorate the half as you wish, including the cut side. I used rolled-out sugar paste, to get a smooth finish. Ice on half the words, and cut one of the candles in half so you can have the correct age!

● HALLOWE'EN SPIDERS ●

I thought it would make a change to have individual cakes, and it's fun for the children to have a spider sitting on every plate. If you want to make a centrepiece instead, you could ice a web on to a cake and put one of these spiders on top. Or you could make a witch by using the Mary Mary technique (opposite), but decorating her with black icing and brown and silver sweets.

For each spider:
1 truffle cake (or roll a round cake in
chocolate vermicelli)
1 liquorice whirl
white icing
chocolate polka dots

1 Unroll the liquorice whirl and cut eight legs of suitable length.
2 Cut two slits on either side of the cake and push the legs into them, squeezing the cake to keep them in place.
3 Add two little blobs of white icing and polka dots for eyes.

● HAT CAKE ●

This would also make a good cake for an Easter party, or a spring birthday. You could add a few flowers (sugar, fabric or even fresh) to the brim, but I quite like the simplicity of the ribbon.

1 20 cm/8 in round sponge cake
2 quantities butter icing
yellow colouring
450 g/1 lb sugar paste
blue colouring
25 cm/10 in cake board

1 Stick the cake to the cake board with a little butter icing, then, if you have one, put the board on to a turntable.
2 Mix a little yellow colouring into the butter icing.
3 Dollop the butter icing roughly all over the cake and board, then spread it with a knife dipped in hot water. When you have it reasonably even, take a fork and mark the 'straw' by pressing the fork into the icing and turning the turntable with the other hand. Start at the centre of the top and work outwards.
4 Colour the sugar paste blue by adding the colouring drop by drop and kneading it in.
5 Roll out the icing, using a little caster sugar to stop it sticking, then cut out a long ribbon. Place it round the cake and make a bow, putting a little paper or cotton wool into the loops of the bow to keep them rounded until they are dry. If you let the ends of the ribbon droop over the brim as I have, you will need to put the cake on a cake stand or turntable so that the ends don't get broken.

● ICE-CREAM CORNETS ●

This idea is entirely due to my four-year-old, Rory. I was spreading the top of the rabbit's head with butter icing, and Rory said to me 'That looks like an ice-cream'. Ah ha! I thought . . . and a new cake was born. You could do endless varieties of ice-cream, and they'd be a good way of carrying cakes around the park or garden at an outdoor party.

doughnuts
butter icing
cornets

Cut a doughnut in half and squeeze one half into the top of a cornet. Spread it liberally with butter icing. This makes the 'vanilla' one.
Variations
Mint choc: Add green colouring, peppermint flavouring and chocolate vermicelli to the icing.
Strawberry: Add strawberry syrup and pink colouring.
Chocolate: Add cocoa powder and a little hot water.
'Soft' ice cream: Swirl the icing up into a peak, and add a chocolate flake.

● IGLOO CAKE ●

It was as I was doing the Beehive (page 90) that the shape suggested an igloo. It makes a change from Christmas trees and snow scenes for a Christmas cake, or it could be funny to have it at an outdoor party on a really hot, sunny day.

1 pudding basin cake
1 quantity butter icing
900 g/2 lb sugar paste
black, red and brown food colouring
icing sugar

1 Colour a little of the sugar paste black, by adding the colouring drop by drop and kneading it in.
2 Cut a small hole out of the bottom edge of the cake, and line it with some of the black icing.
3 Spread the cake with butter icing (or just damp the cake), roll out the white icing, keeping a little set aside, and drape over the cake. Pleat and fold it as necessary to fit, smoothing with damp hands.
4 Mark blocks with the back of a knife.
5 Model some penguins with the black and white icing, and add little yellow eyes.
6 Colour a little icing red and make a Father Christmas, and add a little brown sack.
7 Put the cake on a board, damp it a little and cover with icing sugar.

● MARY MARY CAKE ●

This is more of a meal than a cake, and combines both sweet and savoury courses in one centrepiece. Most children love to eat raw vegetables and salads if offered them, and this way of presenting them makes them irresistible.

1 pudding basin sponge cake
1 quantity butter icing
1 small plastic doll
1 large flat biscuit
sweets and sugar flowers
2 packets of cream cheese
raw vegetable and salads
30 cm/12 in cake board
2 digestive biscuits
coffee beans or nuts

1 Cover the cake with the butter icing. Make a hole in the top.
2 Take the legs off the doll and push her gently into the top of the cake. Add a little icing to her bodice and then press flowers

and sweets all over her 'dress' to decorate.
3 Spread the biscuit with icing and add flowers to the top, then stick it to her head.
4 Place her on the cake board then spread cream cheese thickly all over it. Push the vegetables into the cheese in rows, to make her garden and add a little path of crushed biscuit edged with coffee beans or nuts.

• MINIATURE CAKE •

Either bake a cake in a tiny tin – perhaps a washed fruit or vegetable can? – or cut one out of a large cake with a round cutter. Decorate traditionally.

• MY LITTLE • PONY CASTLE

This beautiful fantasy castle would delight any princess and is much easier to make then it looks. It is a large cake, but as it is made from bought cakes, it cuts down considerably on the construction time.

6 bar cakes any flavour –
try mixing them
4 thin bought swiss rolls
seedless jam
approx 32 penny chews or similar
350 g/¾ lb royal icing
green food colour
1.6 kg/3½ lb sugar paste
4 ice cream cones
35.5 cm/14 in cake board square
25 cm/9 in of 25 mm/1 in wide ribbon
food colour pen
4 plastic straws
small paint brush
small sharp knife
rolling pin
icing sugar
leaf tube
number 2 plain tube
star tube

1 Walls

Cut 2 of the bar cakes in half horizontally. Use the jam to fix each piece on top of the 4 full-size bar cakes. Colour 1.1 kg/2½ lb of the sugar paste pale pink. Cover the walls by rolling out a strip of sugar paste long enough to go all the way round the wall. Spread the sides of the wall with jam and stick sugar paste in position. Cut a small piece to fit the top of the wall, and stick

with jam. Repeat for the other 3 walls. Leave in an upright position while covering the towers.

2 Towers

Trim about 25 mm/1 in off each of the swiss rolls. Roll out a strip of sugar paste long enough to roll round the swiss roll. Cover the sides with jam and roll the sugar paste round the swiss roll. Trim off excess with a sharp knife.

3 To assemble

(1) Place the walls on to the cake board leaving a gap at the corners for the towers. Place the towers in the gaps. When you are sure of a good fit, stick to the board and each other with jam. (2) Use about 225 g/8 oz of the royal icing coloured green to make the grass round the castle. Spread the icing on the board and use a piece of barely damp plastic sponge or the back of a knife pressed into the wet icing to give the rough grass effect.

4 To finish

Cut a template for the windows from a piece of thin card. Make the pink sugar paste darker by adding more colour. Fix in position with water and a small paint brush. Colour 350 g/12 oz of paste blue. Use blue sugar paste to cut out a door and fix to front of the castle.

5 Tower roofs

Use blue semi-circles of sugar paste to cover 4 ice cream cones. Stick with the jam and trim. Cut off about 25 mm/1 in of the point of cone. This leaves a hole to push a straw through. Fix the covered cones to the top of the towers with jam and push a plastic straw through the hole in the cone right down to the bottom till it touches the board. Trim off excess straw, leaving about 4 cm/1½ in. Divide ribbon into 4 and attach to straws to make flags.

6 Battlements

With white royal icing pipe stars along the top back edge of the walls. Push the sweets into the icing leaving a sweet width between each one. Pipe another line of icing along the front edge of walls and repeat the line of sweets.

7 Ivy

Use green icing and a plain icing tube to pipe random lines up the sides of the walls. This helps to cover any gaps where the towers and walls join. Still using green icing but with a leaf tube, pipe leaves on to the stems. Small sweets or coloured icing stars could also be added to make flowers.

8 Lattice windows

Use a food colour pen to mark the windows

with crossed lines to represent lattice windows. Pipe round the windows if desired with white royal icing. Position toys round the castle and on the battlements.

• PIRATE CAKE •

I wanted to make a change from the usual treasure chest and I'm quite pleased with this melodramatic skull and crossbones. The treasure round the side stops it looking too gloomy.

20 cm/8 in round cake (chocolate might
be good, or whatever is the favourite),
split and sandwiched together with
butter icing
1 quantity of butter icing
900 g/2 lb sugar paste
black food colouring
chocolate coins and sweets
small quantity of royal icing

1 Colour most of the sugar paste black, by kneading in the colouring (I recommend wearing rubber gloves – it's a long, messy job).
2 Roll it out, using a little caster sugar to stop it sticking.
3 Either spread the cake with butter icing or simply damp the sugar paste (depending on taste) then cover the cake with the black icing, cutting a strip for the side first then a circle for the top.
4 Blend the join with damp fingers. (Or you can simply place a large circle right over then fold and pleat as necessary to fit.)
5 Roll out and cut a skull and crossbones out of the remainder of the sugar paste and some tiny ones out of the scraps. Stick the large one to the top with a little water, and the small ones to the side.
6 Stick the treasure round the side with a little royal icing.
7 Add pearls made from scraps of sugar paste.

• POSTMAN PAT •

I made a Postman Pat van for Rory's third birthday. It was very pleasant to be making such a gentle character rather than the ferocious types Alexander usually wants – Mr T, Jaws, He-Man and so on. This particular version was made by my friend Janice, and I love the way she's made Jess peeping out of the back.

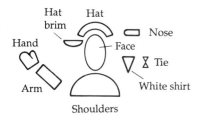

Hat brim Hat Nose Hand Face Tie Arm White shirt Shoulders

Head

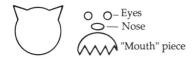

Eyes Nose "Mouth" piece

2 × 20 cm/8 in square sponge cakes
seedless jam
700 g/1½ lb sugar paste
225 g/½ lb butter cream
food colouring red, black, blue, brown
('paste' colours best for strong colours)
royal icing, a small amount coloured
yellow
25 cm/10 in cake board
1 plastic straw
food colouring pen – black

1   Cut each sponge cake in half. Sandwich two pieces together with butter cream. Place the other two pieces on top of each other and cut off about 5 cm/2 in at one end, cutting at a slight angle to form the van windscreen. Sandwich together with butter cream, and fix on to the other two pieces with butter cream. This forms the van shape.
2   Colour 350 g/¾ lb of sugar paste with red. Roll out a strip long enough to cover the front, roof and back of van. Spread a thin layer of jam on the front, roof and back and cover with the red sugar paste. Trim with a sharp knife. Roll two pieces of red to cover the sides of the van, and fix in place with jam.
3   With white sugar paste, cut out the windscreen, two side windows and two small square back windows. Stick in position with water. With a blunt knife or wooden skewer, mark the doors each side and at the back.
4   Colour a small amount of sugar paste black, and cut out 4 small wheels. Fix in position with water. Cut 4 smaller circles in white for the hub caps, and two strips of white for the bumpers, fix in position with water. Cut a rectangle from black sugar paste for the radiator, and mark vertical lines on it with a blunt knife. Fix to front of

van. Cut two small circles of white for the headlamps and fix either side of the radiator.
5   Add a very tiny amount of red to a small piece of white to make it slightly flesh coloured (or use a flesh colour). Colour a small amount of sugar paste blue to make the shoulders and arm for Pat. Model Pat and Jess the cat as shown.
6   Fix Pat to one of the side windows. Jess is fixed to the back by using a small piece of plastic straw pushed into the back window, and gently fixing the head to it. Draw features with food colour pen.
7   Use the cut off pieces of sponge cake to make the mail sacks. Roll out brown sugar paste, spread with jam and wrap round the pieces of sponge cake. This is easier than trying to spread jam on such small pieces of cake.
8   Use a plain icing tube and yellow icing to pipe the words on the side. If you are not very good at piping, you could buy sets of letter cutters which could be used, or just stick a plastic 'Happy Birthday' motto on the side.
9   Candles could be added by pushing the candle holders into the roof.

● RAINBOW CAKE ●

Did you spot my 'deliberate' mistake? I was chatting to the children while I painted this, and got the order of the colours wrong. Oh well, they say every great work of art has a slight imperfection . . .
   When I had made the half cake, I thought I must do something with the left over half. When I stood it on its side, it reminded me of either a bridge or a rainbow. As well as being good for outdoor parties, this would be a lovely cake for a party based on colours, or for a child who loves the Rainbow Brite characters.

1 large round cake (mine was 25 cm/10 in)
900 g/2 lb sugar paste
food colours: red, orange, yellow, green,
blue, indigo, violet
blue paper and white icing to decorate
the board

1   Cut the cake in half, keeping the rest for trifle, or to cut with a round cutter into extra little cakes.
2   Cut a small semi-circle out of the straight side (try to find a saucer or mug to guide you).
3   Roll out the sugar paste, using a little

icing sugar to stop it sticking, and cut strips to cover the cake.
4   When it is dry (just an hour or two will do, but the longer the better), measure the width of the side and divide into seven. Use a compass to mark lightly in pencil (don't worry, it's non-toxic) the arcs. Paint them in with food colouring.
5   Cover a cake board or piece of hardboard with blue shiny paper and pipe on some clouds.

● RED AND GREEN CAKE ●

At first I wasn't sure if this cake was a brilliant work of art or a complete mess, but I've now grown very fond of its Jackson Pollock-like effect. It's enormous fun to do.

1 quantity sponge mix
red and green colouring
1 quantity butter icing
450 g/1 lb sugar paste

1   Make 1 quantity of sponge cake mix and divide it in two.
2   Colour one half red and one half green and bake in two 15 cm/6 in sandwich tins.
3   When cool, sandwich together with the butter icing, coloured red (or green!).
4   Cover with sugar paste and splatter with red and green colouring.

● SCHOOL BOOK ●

Using the rice paper instead of just icing makes this easy to do and has the effect of real pages. This would be a nice un-birthday cake for a child nervous about starting school – make it for tea-time and ask along other little ones who'll be going with him.

2 quantities sponge mix, baked in
28 × 20 cm/11 × 8 in roasting tin
325 g/12 oz sugar paste
red, blue and yellow food colourings
450 g/1 lb icing sugar
2 egg whites
3 large sheets rice paper
blue and red food colouring pens

1   Trim top of cake to resemble an open book.
2   Colour two-thirds of sugar paste red. Roll out to a large rectangle and cover a 36 × 25 cm/14 × 10 in cake board. Trim icing until about 2.5 cm/1 in larger than the cake to make the cover.

3   Place cake on a wire rack set over a tray.
4   Mix sifted icing sugar and egg whites together until smooth. Stir in a little water to give a thick pouring consistency. Spoon over cake and ease down sides. Leave to set. Reserve a little white sugar paste.
5   Colour and shape a rubber and pencil with remainder. Leave to dry.
6   Place cake on red cover.
7   Fold rice paper in half. On one sheet draw pencil lines and letters and a message with food colouring pens. Place on cake securing with reserved sugar paste. Put rubber and pencil on top.

● SEVEN DWARFS CAKE ●

You should really start this a couple of days ahead, to give the headboard and base time to dry. If you're doing it at the last minute you could leave them out – just cover the back with marzipan, drape the beadspread right over the bed, and don't bother to mould any feet.

1 loaf tin cake
1½ packets fondant icing
25 cm/10 in square cake board
7 chocolate finger biscuits
25 oz/½ lb royal icing
7 blue candles
number 1 icing tube
coloured coffee-sugar crystals
1 Club biscuit, or an extra chocolate finger in two pieces

1   Colour ½ packet fondant blue and, remembering you are using the cake widthways, measure and cut pieces to go at the head and the foot of the bed. Leave to dry on non-stick paper. Colour about ¼ packet of fondant flesh pink and make seven little heads and seven pairs of hands and feet, bending hands ready to fit over the top sheet, and marking fingers and toes with a cocktail stick. Leave to dry on non-stick paper.
2   Cover the top of the cake with marzipan and using it widthways place the seven chocolate biscuits across the bed.
3   Colour some little pieces of fondant with various bright colours and wrap round the heads to make hats. Make a pair of slippers in the same colour for each dwarf. Colour a further small piece of fondant brown and make two pick-axes. When dry paint the tops silver. With a no. 1 tube and royal icing, paint glasses onto Doc in silver paint.

4   Paint the faces suitably.
5   Make a long pillow out of white fondant and put it on the bed. Stick the headboard in position and carefully place the candles between this and the pillow. Put the heads on the pillow and stick the feet into a strip of icing at the other end.
6   Put the cake on the board. Colour about ½ packet fondant pink, and measure and cut a bedspread. Drape over the bed making folds at the sides with your fingers.
7   Fold a strip of white fondant over the top edge as a sheet and give Sneezy a handkerchief. Stick the bottom of the bed in position and using a no. 1 tube pipe the beards and hair.
8   Put slippers at the foot of the bed. Colour a small piece of fondant pale brown and wrap it around the biscuit to make a little sack. Put some icing in the top and fill with coffee-sugar 'jewels'. Stick pick-axes as if leaning against the sack.

● SPIDER-MAN CAKE ●

I made this for Alexander's fifth birthday, and when I handed him the knife to make the first slice he neatly chopped off Spider-Man's head! You will have to try to find a toy to copy, as otherwise modelling Spider-Man can be very tricky.

2 quantities of sponge cake mix, baked in a
33 × 25 cm/13 × 10 in roasting tin
675 g/1½ lb icing sugar
3 egg whites
225 g/8 oz sugar paste
red and blue food colourings
100 g/4 oz plain cake covering chocolate

1   Mix sifted icing sugar and egg whites together until smooth. Stir in a little water to give a thick coating consistency. Spoon over cake and ease down sides. Leave to set.
2   Reserve a tiny piece of white sugar paste for eyes and colour remainder red.
3   Model a climbing Spider-Man onto non-stick paper using a child's toy as a guide. Prop Spider-Man's right shoulder and hip with folded paper to make him look as if he is climbing. Leave to dry. Add white icing eyes. Paint markings onto figure using blue food colouring and a fine brush. Leave to dry.
4   Transfer cake to a cake board the same size. Melt chocolate and spoon into a greaseproof paper piping bag fitted with a fine plain tube. Pipe brickwork and a

birthday message onto the cake and leave to dry.
5   Position Spider-Man carefully on the cake.

● SUPERMAN CAKE ●

This run-out technique is extremely useful, and much easier to do than it looks. It can be very good for decorating the top of ice-cream cakes, but remember to make the run-out well ahead, as it will take at least a week to dry. If you haven't time you could trace your design directly onto your cake and do the run-out on top which is much easier.

square cake covered with icing
225–350 g/½–¾ lb royal icing,
depending on the size of picture
several small bowls
non-stick baking parchment or roasting wrap
number 1 and 2 plain icing tubes
nylon or greaseproof icing bags
fine paint brush

1   Any favourite character can be reproduced this way. The most important thing is to find a very clear and simple line drawing to use. Children's colouring book pictures are ideal. If the picture is not quite the right size, your local photocopy shop may be able to reduce or enlarge it for only a few pennies.
2   When you have the correct size picture to fit your cake, fix it on a flat surface with sticky tape. A plastic surfaced tray makes a good base. Cover the picture with a piece of baking parchment or roasting wrap. Roasting wrap is particularly good because it is very clear.
3   Mix up the royal icing to normal consistency, but do NOT add any glycerin, or the icing will not dry out hard enough to be moved. With the number 1 icing tube, outline all the parts of the picture. Mix up several different colours of icing in the small bowls, one for each colour used in the picture. When you have mixed all the colours slowly stir in a little water, drop by drop, until each one is the right consistency. Judge this by letting the icing flow off the spoon or knife and counting how long it takes for the 'trail' to disappear. It should be between 5 and 10 counts. Cover the bowls of icing with a damp cloth or cling film until they are used to prevent the icing from crusting over.
4   Use a number 2 plain icing tube and

one of the thinned coloured icings. Fill the icing bag only half-full. Begin filling in the shapes by outlining the shape and then use a side to side movement working from the top of the shape to the bottom. Fill in all the sections of one particular colour, then leave to dry before filling in the next colour, otherwise the different coloured icings will flow into each other. A small paint brush with a good point helps to push the icing into awkward corners.

5   When all the sections are complete, leave to dry in a warm place. The airing cupboard is ideal. The kitchen is best avoided as a lot of steam is present and the icing may not dry properly.

6   When thoroughly dry, carefully peel off the wax paper or roasting wrap and stick the icing picture on to the cake with a little icing.

Note
Always choose a 'solid' type picture to copy. Thin slender parts are more easily broken. Make a spare 'just in case'!

● THOMAS ●
THE TANK ENGINE

Isn't this brilliant? Janice made this for me, as I'd seen her do one before and was extremely impressed with it. My Thomas that I made a few years ago looked more like a blue slug . . .

*sponge cake approx 25–40 mm/1–1½ in
deep and 28 cm/11 in square
one bought swiss roll
seedless jam
900 g/2 lb sugar paste
food colours, black, blue, red
small amount of royal icing for piping
one cotton wool ball for smoke
food colour pen – black
25 × 30 cm/10 × 12 in cake board
(finished size of cake
10 × 25 cm/4 × 10 in)
plain biscuit cutter, approx 5 cm/2 in
diameter
225 g/½ lb butter cream
number 3 icing tube
small sharp knife
rolling pin
icing sugar for 'rolling out'
rounded end modelling tool (or knitting
needle or similar)*

1   Method
The basic shapes are cut from sponge, covered with sugar paste, and then

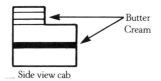
Side view cab — Butter Cream

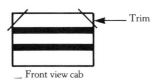
Front view cab — Trim

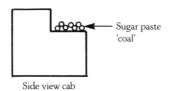
Side view cab — Sugar paste 'coal'

assembled. Colour 450 g/1 lb sugar paste blue, 225 g/8 oz grey, 100 g/4 oz black, 100 g/4 oz red. Save a small piece of white for eyeballs.

2   Base
Cut out 2 base shapes 9 × 23 cm/ 3½ × 9 in. Sandwich together with butter cream. Spread the top and sides with a thin layer of jam. Roll out the grey sugar paste (save a small piece for the face) and cover the top and sides 'all in one'. Trim excess with a sharp knife. Save trimmings to help make the face.

3   Boiler
Use a thin supermarket swiss roll. Trim to 12.5 cm/5 in long. Roll out some blue sugar paste large enough to cover the roll lengthways. Spread jam on the sides of the swiss roll, and roll it up in the blue sugar paste. Trim. Cut and fix a large piece of blue sugar paste to fit the raised back of cab.

4   Cab
Cut two cab shapes and one cab roof. (1) Sandwich all three together with butter cream. Spread the sides with jam. Cover the sides with a strip of blue sugar paste long enough to go all the way round the sides. For neatness make the join at a corner. Trim. Cut and fix a piece of blue sugar paste to cover the raised back of cab. (2) Trim the cab roof with a sharp knife to make it slightly curved. Cover with a strip of black sugar paste. Spread the coal tender part of cab with jam. (3) Pull off small

pieces of black sugar paste from a larger piece to make rough coal shapes, and stick on to the jam.

5   Tanks
Cut out two tank shapes. These may need to be cut slightly thinner depending on the thickness of the swiss roll. Check the fit on the base before covering with the blue sugar paste. Spread jam on the base, top and sides of each tank and cover 'all in one'. Trim with a sharp knife.

6   To assemble
Fix the base to board with a little jam. Fix the cab on to the base at one end. Fix boiler on to base and butt up to the cab. Position tanks either side of the boiler, and stick with jam.

7   Wheels
Use a biscuit cutter to cut the 8 wheels from blue sugar paste, the same height as the base. Stick to the sides of the base, 4 each side.

8   To finish
Cut window shapes for the cab from black sugar paste. Two small circles for the front of the cab, and two squares for the sides. Fix in position. Make a blue dome shape from blue sugar paste and fix in place on the boiler. Roll out a strip of red sugar paste, about 6 mm/¼ in thick and 12mm × 9cm/½ × 3½ in long for the front and back of the base. Make 4 small buffers from black sugar paste and fix to the red strip, 2 for the front and 2 for the back. Roll a strip of red sugar paste approx 12 mm/½ in wide and the length of the base and fix in position over the top of the wheels on one side. Repeat for the other side.

9   Face
The most important part. It helps to have a picture of Thomas to copy. Roll out the grey sugar paste quite thick, approx 12 mm/½ in, and cut out a circle the same diameter as the boiler. Leave the sugar paste in the cutter if possible as this helps to stop the face 'spreading' when the eyes are pushed in. Indent the eye sockets with the blunt end of a wooden skewer, or a round ended modelling tool or similar object. Roll two small eyeballs of white sugar paste, dampen the eye socket with a little water, and fix them in position. For the nose, roll a small ball of grey sugar paste and stick with water. Use a modelling tool or your little finger to make the cheeks slightly rounded. Mark a smiling mouth with a sharp knife. Use the black food colour pen to mark the eyeballs and

eyebrows. Remove the cutter and if possible leave to dry overnight. Stick the face to the front of the boiler with a little jam. Roll a strip of black sugar paste 25 mm/1 in wide and long enough to go round the boiler. Fix in position where the face joins the boiler. Make a black sugar paste chimney, stick to boiler with water. Use a cotton wool ball for the smoke by pulling it into shape. Push into top of chimney.

10 Use red coloured royal icing and a plain icing tube to pipe the lines on the tanks and boiler.

Note

If not very good at piping try using thin strips of red sugar paste or red 'bootlace' sweets cut into the right length and stuck in place with water.

• THREE BEARS •

I told my daughter Katie the story of Goldilocks and the Three Bears over and over again when she was three, and it's been a favourite of mine ever since. Nursery rhymes are always good sources of inspiration for cakes.

2 quantities of sponge mix, baked in a
18 × 26 × 4 cm/7 × 11 × 1 in tin
900 g/2 lb sugar paste
yellow and green food colourings
1 tbsp apricot jam
100 g/4 oz marzipan
blue, black and red food colouring pens
3 candles

1 Cut sponge into three beds of decreasing size.

2 Roll out one-quarter of the icing thinly and use to cover a 36 × 47.5 cm/14 × 19in cake board. Trim to make a carpet and paint yellow. Place cakes on cake board. Brush beds with jam. Roll out icing to cover top third of each bed.

3 Shape 3 pillows and place on iced portions.

4 Make body shapes from icing and place on beds.

5 Roll out bedspreads, position on beds and trim.

6 Add icing strips for sheets.

7 Shape three bears' heads and paws from marzipan and leave to dry. Paint features on bears.

8 Position on cake. Add patterns to bedclothes and carpet with brushed on

food colourings and pens. Add candles if liked.

• TRANSFORMER CAKE •

This is a useful technique for making all sorts of shapes. It's much better to cut out and build up an unusual design, rather than spend your time searching the country for a Gobot or Transepticon cake tin . . .

30 cm/12 in square sponge cake approx
4 cm/1½ in deep
cake board 30 × 40 cm/12 × 16 in, or
40 cm/16 in square
225 g/½ lb butter cream (if required)
700 g/1½ lb sugar paste
seedless jam
red, blue and black food colours
small paint brush
optional: brilliant edible silver powder
(see below)
thin card (cereal packet) for templates

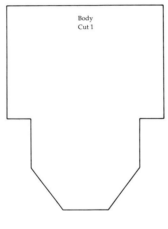

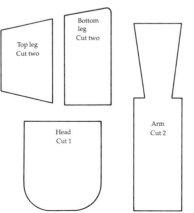

1 If wished, slice the cake in half horizontally, and sandwich together with butter cream. As the cake is not very deep it can be left plain.

2 Cut out the basic shapes from thin card. Arrange the shapes on the sponge cake and cut out with a sharp knife. This method is more economical than trying to cut out the full size shape all in one. Any left over pieces can be eaten by the children or saved in the freezer.

3 Divide the sugar paste into half. Colour one half red. Divide the other half into two. Colour one piece blue, and using a little black colour, make the other piece grey.

4 Spread the arm parts with jam top and sides only. Cover 'all in one' with red sugar paste. Trim with a sharp knife. Cover upper part of body in the same way. Use grey sugar paste to cover the lower body and upper leg parts. Head and lower legs are covered with the blue sugar paste. Arrange pieces on the board using jam to fix into position.

5 Use the blue sugar paste trimmings to shape the hands and feet and add the features to the head. Use the grey trimmings to cut out the body decoration. Cut small wheel shapes from the grey and stick with water on the sides of the body. Cut 4 slightly smaller wheels also in grey and fix two to each side of the lower legs with water.

6 To give a more metallic look to the grey parts, use EDIBLE silver powder food colouring. This can be mixed with a tiny amount of water and painted on to the grey sugar paste with a small paint brush. If this is not available, the grey on its own looks quite effective.

• UPSIDE DOWN CAKE •

I originally imagined balancing the cake on its candles, but we found they just weren't strong enough to support the weight. Janice came up with the idea of supporting it on a wedding cake pillar and cake board, which works very well.

20 cm/8 in round sponge cake,
home made or bought, traditionally iced
15 cm/6 in round thin cake board
75 cm/3 in cake pillar
strong glue, e.g. Bostic
birthday candles and holders

1 With the glue, stick the cake pillar on to the middle of the small cake board.

Allow to dry.

2　Stick the cake board on to the centre of the cake with icing or jam.

3　Push the candle holders into the cake round the cake board. Melt the bottom of each candle and fix into the candle holders to stop them falling out when turned upside down.

4　Turn the cake upside down on to the table or plate, so that it rests on the pillar.

Note

If a cake board is stuck to the bottom of the cake with a little icing or jam, it makes it easier to turn the cake the right way up again to be cut.

NOTES ON MEASUREMENTS AND AMERICAN RECIPE GLOSSARY

Use either metric, imperial or American measurements in any one recipe, as the systems are not exact equivalents.

Almond niblets can be replaced by slivered almonds, lightly chopped.

Beef mince, or minced beef, is ground beef.

Bicarbonate of soda is baking soda.

Biscuits are cookies if sweet, crackers if savory.

Biscuit cutter is a cookie cutter.

Bootlace sweets are like thin licorice strings.

Caster sugar is more finely ground than British granulated sugar; for both substitute US granulated white sugar.

Chips are French fries.

Chocolate drops are chocolate chips.

Chocolate Flake is a small chocolate candy baton.

Cling film is plastic wrap.

Clotted cream is much thicker than heavy cream, but heavy cream can be used as a substitute.

Coffee essence is coffee extract.

Cotton wool ball is a cotton ball.

Custard powder, a cornflour mixture, is available in the US at specialty food shops.

Demerara sugar is granulated brown sugar; use white sugar instead.

Double cream is heavy cream; if unavailable, use whipping cream.

Digestive biscuits are best replaced by Graham crackers.

Frozen lollies (banana, cherry, etc) are the same idea as 'Popsicles'.

Fruit jelly is a 'Jello'-type dessert.

Gelatine is gelatin.

Glacé cherries are candied cherries.

Golden syrup can be substituted with light corn syrup.

Greaseproof paper is wax paper.

Grill is broil or broiler.

Grilled is broiled.

Icing sugar is confectioners' sugar.

Marmite can be replaced by Bovril.

Muesli is like Bircher Muesli breakfast cereal.

Muscovado sugar is best replaced by dark brown sugar.

Paper cases are cupcake cases if large, fine chocolate candy cases if small.

Penny sweets are small hard candies.

Plain chocolate is semi-sweet chocolate.

Plain flour is all-purpose flour.

Polythene bag is plastic bag.

Popcorn is popping corn.

Royal icing is 'royal glaze icing', a mixture of egg white, confectioners' sugar and sometimes a few drops of glycerin to make it less hard.

Sandwich tin can be substituted by a round layer cake pan of appropriate size.

Scones are like US biscuits.

Shrimps are shrimp.

Sponge cake can be substituted by pound cake.

Stock cube is bouillon cube.

Sugar paste is

Swiss roll/tin is jelly roll/pan.

Toad-in-the-hole is pig-in-blanket.

Tomato purée is tomato paste.

Vanilla essence is vanilla extract.

Yorkshire pudding tins are unavailable; use a cupcake pan instead, but fill only one-third full.

RECIPES

Ideas for sandwich fillings

Avocado mashed with a little
lemon juice

Mashed banana

Chopped hard-boiled egg and
mayonnaise

Marmite and cream cheese

Ham, puréed with cream cheese

Chopped walnuts and cream cheese

Tuna fish and mayonnaise

Cucumber

Smoked salmon pieces and
cream cheese

Shrimp and pink mayonnaise

Sardines mashed with a little
lemon juice

Date, cream cheese and honey

BLT Bacon, lettuce and tomato

Club sandwiches, made with bacon,
chicken or turkey, lettuce and tomato

Sliced tomato and grated cheese

Chopped chicken and mayonnaise

Use brown or white bread, bridge rolls,
French bread, 'swiss rolls' using brown or
white bread, pitta bread

Open sandwiches (use crispbread for diet-
conscious 12-year-olds)

Use toasted bread for BLTs and Club
sandwiches

Open 'toasted' sandwiches. (Toast bread
on one side, cover untoasted side with
ham, cooked chicken or tomato, etc, top
with grated cheese and grill)

Sliced bread sandwiches can be cut into
animal shapes once filled, or gingerbread
men cutters

Fillings for Baked Potatoes

Shrimps and pink seasoned
cream cheese

Home-made baked beans

Chili con carne

Shepherd's pie potatoes (i.e. scoop out
the inside of baked potato, half fill
with shepherd's pie recipe, top with
potato – and grated cheese if wished)

Grated cheese and crumble crispy
bacon

Chopped cooked chicken,
mushrooms and cream

Cream cheese and chopped chives

Sweetcorn, peas and chopped
red pepper

• CHEESE SCONES •

Makes 18 to 20

*225 g/8 oz/2 cups self raising flour
1.25 ml/¼ tsp salt
25 g/1 oz/2 tbsp butter
100 g/4 oz/1 cup Cheddar cheese,
finely grated
150 ml/¼ pt/⅔ cup milk*

1   Pre-heat oven to 220°C/425°F/ gas 7.
2   Sift the flour and salt together. Rub in
the butter until the mixture resembles fine
breadcrumbs. Add 75 g/3 oz/¾ cup of the
grated cheese to the mixture and bind
together with the milk to form a soft
dough.
3   On a floured surface roll out to
15 mm/½ in thick and cut into rounds
with a pastry cutter 4 cm/1½ in in
diameter.
4   Place on a lightly greased baking sheet.
Brush with milk and sprinkle with remaining grated cheese. Bake for 12 minutes.
5   Cool on a wire rack.

Note
This can be made in a food processor but
will take slightly less milk.

• CHIVE BISCUITS •

Makes 12

*100 g/4 oz/1 cup self raising wholemeal
flour
1.25 ml/¼ tsp salt
25 g/1 oz/2 tbsp butter, cubed
1 bunch chopped chives
50 ml/2 fl oz/¼ cup milk*

1   Pre-heat the oven to 200°C/400°F/ gas
mark 6.
2   Sift the flour with the salt. Rub in the
butter until crumbly and stir the chopped
chives and milk into the mixture with a
fork. Form into a soft ball.
3   Turn out on to a lightly floured surface

and knead. Roll out to 12 mm/ ½ in thick
and cut into 5 cm/2 in rounds with a pastry
cutter. Place on a greased baking sheet.
Brush with melted butter and bake for 15
minutes.
4   Cool on a wire rack.

Note
This recipe can be made in a food
processor – in which case use slightly less
milk.

• RUSKS •

Makes 24

*225 g/8 oz/2 cups self raising flour
pinch of salt
50 g/2 oz/4 tbsp butter
1 mediumsized egg, beaten
45 ml/3 tbsp milk*

1   Pre-heat oven to 220°C/425°F/ gas 7.
2   Sieve the flour and salt into a bowl. Cut
the butter into small pieces and rub into
the flour until the texture resembles fine
breadcrumbs. Add the beaten egg and
milk and knead into a soft dough.
3   Roll out 12 mm/½ in thick on a lightly
floured surface and cut into rounds with a
5 cm/2 in plain cutter. Place rounds on a
lightly greased baking tray.
4   Bake for 10–15 minutes or until well
risen and lightly browned.
5   Remove from oven and cool slightly.
Split the rusks in half and return to the
oven for 15 minutes at 160°C/325°F/gas 3
or until brown at the edges with crisp
golden centres.
6   Cool rusks on a wire rack.

• STILTON BISCUITS •

Makes approx 24

*125 g/4 oz/½ cup, tightly packed
Stilton
100 g/4 oz/½ cup softened butter
1 medium-sized egg, separated
175 g/6 oz/1½ cups flour*

1   Pre-heat oven to 220°C/425°F/ gas 7.
2   Scrape all the rind off the cheese. Put it
into a mixing bowl with the butter and
mash together until well blended. Work
the egg yolk evenly into the cheese

mixture. Work in the flour gradually, using
a fork at first and then your hand until you
have a very soft dough. Wrap in cling film
and chill for 30 minutes or until firm.
3 Roll out dough to 5 mm/¼ in thick on
a lightly floured surface and cut into
rounds or shapes. Place biscuits on a lightly
greased baking sheet. Lightly beat the egg
white and brush this over the biscuits.
4 Bake for 12 to 15 minutes or until
lightly browned.
5 Cool on a wire rack.

Note
This can be made in a food processor.

• BASIC BISCUIT DOUGH No. 1 •

Makes 18

100 g/4 oz/8 tbsp butter
50 g/2 oz/¼ cup caster sugar
175 g/6 oz/1¼ cups plain flour

1 Pre-heat oven to 150°C/300°F/ gas 2.
2 Cream the butter and the sugar until
pale and fluffy.
3 Work in the sifted flour and knead
lightly into a ball. Roll out 5 mm/⅛ in
thick on a lightly floured surface. Cut into
shapes with biscuit cutters and prick each
biscuit with a fork.
4 Bake in the centre of the oven for about
25 minutes.
5 Cool on a wire rack and decorate as
required.

Note
This can be made in a food processor.

• BASIC BISCUIT DOUGH No. 2 •

Makes 24 to 30

100 g/4 oz/8 tbsp butter or margarine
25 g/1 oz/¼ cup icing sugar
100 g/4 oz/1 cup plain flour, sifted

1 Pre-heat the oven to 160°C/325°F/ gas
mark 3.
2 In a deep bowl beat the butter with a
wooden spoon until creamy. Add the sifted
icing sugar and beat until the mixture is
pale and fluffy.
3 Stir in the sifted flour to give a soft
dough.

4 Pipe or spoon on to 2 greased baking
trays 25 mm/1 in apart; the biscuits spread.
If piping use a medium vegetable nozzle.
5 Bake in the centre of the oven for about
25 minutes or until pale golden.
6 Cool on a wire rack.

Variation
½ glacé cherry can be put in the centre of
each piped biscuit before baking.

Note
This recipe can be made using a food
processor.

• CHOCOLATE CHIP COOKIES •

Makes 18 to 24

100 g/4 oz/8 tbsp butter
75 g/3 oz/generous ⅓ cup, packed soft brown sugar
1 medium-sized egg
150 g/5 oz/1¼ cups plain flour
2.5 ml/½ tsp salt
0.5 ml/1 tsp bicarbonate of soda
75 g/3 oz/⅓ cup chocolate drops

1 Pre-heat the oven to 180°C/350°F/ gas
mark 4.
2 Cream the butter and the sugar in a
bowl until light and fluffy. Beat in the egg
until well mixed. Sift in the flour, salt and
bicarbonate of soda and mix well. Fold in
the chocolate drops.
3 Drop spoonfuls of dough on to a
lightly greased baking sheet, keeping well
apart as the mixture spreads while cooking.
4 Bake for 10 minutes or until pale
golden.
5 Cool on a wire rack.

• CHOCOLATE CORNFLAKE CRISPIES •

Makes 24 minis or 12 maxis

175 g/6 oz/12 tbsp butter
50 g/2 oz/scant ¼ cup, packed soft brown sugar
30 ml/2 tbsp golden syrup
45 ml/3 tbsp cocoa powder
175 g/6 oz/6 cups cornflakes
(break up flakes for mini crispies)

1 Melt butter, sugar and syrup in a large

saucepan over a low heat until well
blended.
2 Remove from heat and mix in sifted
cocoa powder. Allow to cool slightly and
add cornflakes, mixing well so that cornflakes are completely coated.
3 Heap into large or small paper cases
and allow to cool.

• CRUNCHIES •

Makes 24 to 30 minis

3 Mars bars
100 g/4 oz/8 tbsp butter
50 g/2 oz/2 cups Rice Crispies

1 Cut Mars bars into small pieces and
put into a saucepan with the butter. Stir
over a low heat until melted. Quickly
remove from heat (be careful as this gets
very hot) and add Rice Crispies, coating
well.
2 Put mixture into mini paper cases
before it sets.

• FORTUNE COOKIES •

Makes approx 12 cookies

50 g/2 oz/¼ cup sugar
2 medium-sized egg whites, unbeaten
pinch of salt
50 g/2 oz/4 tbsp melted butter
50 g/2 oz/½ cup plain flour
1.25 ml/¼ tsp vanilla essence

1 Pre-heat oven to 180°C/350°F/ gas 4.
2 Prepare 'fortunes' on 6 × 1 cm/
2½ in × ½ in slips of paper.
3 In a mixing bowl stir the sugar into the
egg whites. Add a pinch of salt. When the
sugar is dissolved add the butter, flour and
vanilla and beat until smooth.
4 Drop the batter, 5 ml/1 tsp at a time,
on to a greased baking tray, making sure
that they are at least 5 cm/2 in apart.
5 Bake for 5 minutes or until the edges
are brown.
6 Remove immediately from oven, place
a 'fortune' across the centre of each circle
and fold over into a semi-circle. Now lay
the semi-circle over the edge of a mixing
bowl and hold for a few seconds until it
holds its shape.
7 Keep working fast until all the cookies
are made!

● GINGERBREAD MEN ●

Makes 12 to 14

350 g/12 oz/3 cups plain flour
5 ml/1 tsp ground allspice
5 ml/1 tsp ground ginger
5 ml/1 tsp ground cinnamon
pinch of salt
2.5 ml/1/2 tsp bicarbonate of soda
175 g/6 oz/12 tbsp butter
60 ml/4 tbsp soft dark brown sugar
120 ml/8 tbsp golden syrup
90 ml/6 tbsp milk
currants
glacé cherries, finely sliced

1   Sift the flour, spices, salt and bicarbonate of soda into a large mixing bowl.
2   In another large bowl beat the butter with a wooden spoon until soft. Add the sugar and golden syrup and beat continuously until light and fluffy.
3   With a metal spoon fold the flour mixture alternately with the milk into the butter mixture.
4   Once blended knead until smooth. Wrap the dough in cling film and chill overnight.
5   Heat the oven to 190°C/375°F/ gas 5.
6   Roll out the dough to 3 mm/1/8 in thick on a lightly floured surface. Using a floured gingerbread-man cutter approx. 15 cm/6 in long, cut out 12 to 14 shapes. Arrange the gingerbread men on 2 or 3 lightly greased baking trays and decorate with currants for eyes and buttons and finely sliced glacé cherries (cut in half) for smiles.
7   Bake in the oven for 15 minutes or until golden and firm to the touch.
8   Cool on a wire rack.

● JEWELLED BISCUITS ●

Makes 12

100 g/4 oz/1/2 cup butter
50 g/2 oz/1/4 cup caster sugar
175 g/6 oz/11/2 cups plain flour, sifted
45 ml/3 tbsp jam

1   Pre-heat oven to 150°C/300°F/ gas 2.
2   Cream the butter and the sugar until pale and fluffy. Work in the sifted flour and knead lightly into a ball. On a lightly floured surface roll out to 3 mm/1/8 in thick.
3   Using a fluted 5 cm/2 in biscuit cutter cut out 24 rounds. With a 25 mm/1 in

cutter cut a hole in the centre of 12 of the rounds. Spread the plain rounds with jam, place the cut rounds on top and press gently together.
4   Bake in the centre of the oven for about 25 minutes.
5   Cool on a wire rack.

Note
These look very pretty if icing sugar is dusted over them shortly before serving. This can be made in a food processor.

● MUESLI BARS ●

Makes approximately 16

100 g/4 oz butter
75 g/3 oz soft brown sugar
45 ml/3 tbsp golden syrup
175 g/6 oz muesli
100 g/4 oz Fruit and Fibre

1   Pre-heat the oven to 180°C/350°F/ gas mark 4.
2   In a deep saucepan melt the butter, demerara sugar and golden syrup.
3   Add muesli and Fruit and Fibre and mix until well coated.
4   Grease a swiss roll tin 22.5 × 35 cm/ 9 × 14 in and spread the mixture in the tin.
5   Bake for about 15 minutes until golden brown and bubbling.
6   Remove from oven, and when slightly cooled mark into slices. When cold cut into slices and turn out.

Note
Muesli and Fruit and Fibre are not available in America, so American measurements have not been given for this recipe.

● PINK MERINGUES ●

Makes 24

1 medium-sized egg white
50 g/2 oz/1/4 cup caster sugar
few drops pink food colouring

1   Pre-heat the oven to 170°C/325°F/ gas mark 3.
2   Beat the egg white until stiff. Beat in half the sugar 15 ml/1 tbsp at a time. Fold in the remaining sugar and a few drops of pink colouring.
3   Pipe on to non-stick paper and cook in the turned-off oven overnight.

● SWEET POPCORN ●

175 g/6 oz/1 cup popcorn kernels
15 ml/1 tbsp vegetable oil
450 g/1 lb/2 cups sugar
105 ml/7 tbsp golden syrup
100 g/4 oz/8 tbsp butter
2.5 ml/1/2 tsp cream of tartar
2.5–5 ml/1/2–1 tsp food colouring

1   In a large heavy bottomed saucepan stir the popcorn in the oil to coat. Cover the pan and turn on high heat. Shake as corn pops to prevent it burning and continue shaking until all popping noises have stopped. Put popcorn in a large bowl.
2   In a large heavy saucepan mix sugar, golden syrup, butter and cream of tartar. Cook over a low heat until melted. Continue cooking without stirring until the temperature reaches 121°C/250°F or until a sample tested in cold water forms a hard ball. Add food colouring and remove from heat.
3   Pour syrup slowly over the popcorn, tossing with lightly oiled spoons to mix. This is best done with 2 people.
4   Spread out on a tray to cool.

Note
This can be made up to 2 days in advance and stored in an airtight container.

● SUGAR-FREE ●
TRUFFLES

Makes 12

50 g/2 oz/8 tbsp butter
few drops artificial liquid sweetener
75 g/3 oz/1/3 cup ground almonds
5 ml/1 tsp cocoa powder
50 g/2 oz/1/2 cup cake crumbs
(made from sugar-free sponge recipe)
15–30 ml/1–2 tbsp orange juice
25–50 g/1–2 oz almond niblets

1   Cream the butter and the sweetener until light and fluffy. Add the ground almonds and cocoa powder. Blend thoroughly. Mix in sufficient cake crumbs to form a stiff paste. Add orange juice.
2   Form mixture into 12 balls and coat these in the almond niblets. Keep in a cool place until required.

• WHOLE GLACÉ • STRAWBERRIES

225 g/8 oz/1²/₃ cups strawberries,
not hulled
225 g/8 oz/1 cup sugar
150 ml/¹/₄ pt/²/₃ cup water
pinch of cream of tartar
dissolved in a little water

1 Wipe the strawberries – do not hull them.
2 In a small heavy-based saucepan dissolve the sugar in the water over low heat. Add the dissolved cream of tartar, bring to the boil and boil rapidly to the hard crack stage or 160°C/300°F on a sugar thermometer. To test, drop a little syrup in a saucer of cold water – it will be very hard. Stop cooking by dipping the base of the pan in cold water. As soon as the bubbles have subsided dip each strawberry in separately, holding it by the stem. Drain slightly and place on a greased baking tray. Ensure that each strawberry is completely coated. Leave to set.
3 Serve individually, perhaps in mini paper cases.

Note
These can be prepared 2 to 3 hours in advance but they must be kept in a cool, dry place to prevent them becoming sticky. Just before serving place them in the paper cases.

• BANANA WACKY • CAKE

Makes 12 slices

100 g/4 oz/1 cup self raising
wholemeal flour
100 g/4 oz/¹/₄ cup sifted plain flour
5 ml/1 tsp baking powder
1.25 ml/¹/₄ tbsp bicarbonate of soda
1.25 ml/¹/₄ tsp mixed spice
50 g/2 oz/4 tbsp butter
1 medium-sized egg
75 g/3 oz/²/₃ cup dried, stoned
chopped dates
3 bananas, mashed
50 ml/2 fl oz/¹/₄ cup milk
100 g/4 oz/²/₃ cup soft brown sugar

1 Pre-heat oven to 180°C/350°F/ gas 4.
2 Mix together the dry ingredients.
3 Using a wooden spoon cream the butter with the sugar. Add the egg and beat well. Stir in the dates and mashed bananas. Fold in the flour mixture alter-

nately with the milk.
4 Spread the mixture evenly in a greased round 20 cm/8 in/10 cup cake tin and bake for 1 hour or until an inserted skewer comes out clean.
5 Turn cake out of the tin and cool on a wire rack.

• BASIC SPONGE •

175 g/6 oz/³/₄ cup butter or margarine, or
a mixture of both
175 g/6 oz/³/₄ cup caster sugar
3 eggs
175 g/6 oz/³/₄ cup self-raising flour

Heat the oven to 190°C/375°F/gas 5 and either line your tin(s) with baking parchment or grease very thoroughly. Cream the butter (or margarine) together until light and fluffy. Add the beaten egg little by little, beating well after each addition. Fold in the flour then turn into your prepared tin(s).
Bake in the centre of the oven for 20 to 25 minutes. When the cake feels springy in the middle when pressed it is ready. Take it out of the oven and after a minute or two run a knife round the edge before turning it onto a wire tray to cool.

• CHOCOLATE • BROWNIES

100 g/4 oz/8 tbsp butter
75 g/3 oz/²/₃ cup plain flour
40 g/1¹/₂ oz/¹/₃ cup cocoa powder
2 medium-sized eggs, lightly beaten
225 g/8 oz/1 cup caster sugar
finely grated zest of 1 orange

1 Pre-heat the oven to 180°C/350°F/ gas mark 4.
2 Melt the butter in a small pan and leave it until lukewarm.
3 Sift together the flour and cocoa powder.
4 Beat the eggs and sugar together until light and fluffy. Fold in the flour, cocoa, melted butter and orange zest until evenly mixed.
5 Turn the mixture into a greased 18 cm/7 in square tin and spread it smoothly.
6 Bake for 25 to 30 minutes until springy to the touch.
7 Leave to cool in the tin. Once cold turn out on to a wire rack and ice with Chocolate Fudge Icing, if desired.

• CHOCOLATE • FUDGE CAKE

225 g/8 oz wholewheat plain digestive
biscuits
20 ml/4 tsp cocoa powder
100 g/4 oz butter
60 ml/2 tbsp golden syrup
100 g/4 oz Chocolate Eclairs
(toffee-coated chocolate sweets)
1 recipe Chocolate Fudge Icing,
see page 000

1 Line an 18 cm/7 in sandwich tin with greaseproof paper.
2 Crumble biscuits in the blender or crush with a rolling pin between 2 sheets of greaseproof paper. Stir in the cocoa.
3 Melt the butter and syrup in a deep pan. Add the toffees and continue melting over a very low heat. When melted add the crushed biscuits and mix well.
4 Press into the sandwich tin and leave to cool before turning out.
5 Cover with chocolate fudge icing.

Note
As Chocolate Eclairs are not available in America, American measurements have been omitted.

• CHOCOLATE • NUT SQUARES

Makes 16

50 g/2 oz/¹/₂ cup plain flour
1.25 ml/¹/₄ tsp salt
75 g/3 oz/¹/₃ cup plain chocolate or
chocolate drops
25 g/1 oz/2 tbsp unsalted butter
2 medium-sized eggs
75 g/3 oz/scant ¹/₃ cup muscovado
sugar
75 g/3 oz/³/₄ cup coarsely chopped
walnuts or pecans

1 Pre-heat the oven to 180°C/350°F/ gas mark 4.
2 Sift together the flour and the salt.
3 Melt the chocolate with the butter over a low heat and cool slightly.
4 Beat the eggs and sugar until light and fluffy. Beat in the chocolate mixture and then the dry ingredients. Mix well and stir in the nuts. Pour into an 18 cm/7 in greased square tin.
5 Bake for 20 to 25 minutes or until an inserted skewer comes out clean.
6 Leave in the tin until almost cool before cutting into squares.

• COFFEE CAKE •

12 slices

175 g/6 oz/³⁄₄ cup butter
175 g/6 oz/³⁄₄ cup caster sugar
4 medium-sized eggs
25 ml/6 oz/1¹⁄₂ cups self raising flour,
sifted
25 ml/1¹⁄₂ tbsp coffee essence

1   Pre-heat the oven to 190°C/375°F/ gas mark 5.
2   Cream the butter and sugar until light and fluffy. Beat the eggs and add to the creamed butter gradually, beating the mixture well. Beat in the coffee essence. Fold in the flour, mixing to a soft dropping consistency with a little warm water if necessary.
3   Divide the mixture beween 2 greased 18 cm/7 in sandwich tins. Bake in the centre of the oven for 20 minutes or until well risen.
4   Turn cakes out of the tins and cool on a wire rack.

• FRUIT CAKE •

Makes 12 slices

150 g/5 oz/²⁄₃ cup caster sugar
150 g/5 oz/²⁄₃ cup butter
3 medium-sized eggs
175 g/6 oz/1¹⁄₂ cups plain flour
100 g/4 oz/³⁄₄ cup currants
100 g/4 oz/³⁄₄ cup sultanas

1   Pre-heat oven to 180°C/350°F/ gas 4.
2   In a large bowl cream together the butter and sugar until light and fluffy. Beat in the eggs one at a time, then half the sifted flour. Then add half the dried fruit, the remaining flour and the rest of the fruit.
3   Pour into a buttered and floured round 20 cm/8 in/10 cup cake tin and bake for 1 hour or until an inserted skewer comes out clean.
4   Turn cake out of tin and cool on a wire rack.

• SUGAR-FREE • SPONGE CAKE

Makes 12 slices

100 g/4 oz/¹⁄₂ cup butter or margarine
2.5 ml/¹⁄₂ tsp vanilla essence
10 ml/2 tbsp liquid artificial sweetener
25 g/1 oz/¹⁄₄ cup wholemeal self raising
flour
2 medium-sized eggs
200 g/7 oz/1³⁄₄ cup white self raising
flour
150 ml/6 fl oz/³⁄₄ cup milk

1   Pre-heat the oven to 180°C/350°F/ gas mark 4.
2   Cream the butter until pale. Add the vanilla, sweetener and wholemeal flour. Beat well.
3   Add the eggs, one at a time, beating well after each addition.
4   Fold in the rest of the flour alternately with the milk, beginning and ending with the flour.
5   Pour into a greased loaf tin or 18 cm/7 in square cake tin.
6   Bake for 30 to 35 minutes or until well risen and golden brown.
7   Cool on a wire rack.

Variations
ORANGE CAKE
Omit vanilla essence. Add finely grated zest and juice of 1 orange with sufficient milk to make up to the 150 ml/6 fl oz/ ³⁄₄ cup liquid.
CHOCOLATE CAKE
Sift 30 ml/2 tbsp cocoa powder with the flour. Add more milk if the batter is too dry.

• RICH • CHOCOLATE CAKE

12 slices

175 g/6 oz/³⁄₄ cup butter
175 g/6 oz/³⁄₄ cup caster sugar
4 medium-sized eggs, separated
175 g/6 oz/³⁄₄ cup plain chocolate or
chocolate drops, melted and cooled
100 g/4 oz/1 cup plain flour

1   Pre-heat the oven to 180°C/350°F/ gas mark 4.
2   Cream the butter and sugar together until light and fluffy. Beat in the egg yolks and cooled chocolate. Fold in the sifted flour. In another bowl beat the egg whites until they form soft peaks and fold these

into the mixture.
3   Divide the mixture between two 18 cm/7 in sandwich tins which have been greased. Bake for approximately 20 minutes or until well risen.
4   Turn out and cool on a wire rack.

• BLACKCURRANT • YOGHURT SODA

Serves 1

30 ml/2 tbsp concentrated blackcurrant
or other concentrated fruit juice
150 ml/5 fl oz/²⁄₃ cup fizzy mineral water
75 ml/3 fl oz/¹⁄₃ cup plain low-fat yoghurt
0 ml/2 tbsp vanilla ice cream

1   Put the blackcurrant juice, mineral water, yoghurt and half the ice cream into a blender and work them into a frothy liquid.
2   Pour the drink into a glass and top with the remaining ice cream.

• MINT MILKSHAKE •

2 scoops mint ice cream
150 ml/¹⁄₄ pt/²⁄₃ cup milk
green food colouring (if necessary)
sprig of mint for decoration

Blend ingredients together in a blender and serve in a tall glass decorated with mint sprig.

• RASPBERRY • YOGHURT SHAKE

Serves 1

100 ml/4 fl oz/¹⁄₂ cup milk
100 ml/4 fl oz/¹⁄₂ cup plain low-fat
yoghurt
45 ml/3 tbsp raspberry syrup
1 scoop raspberry ice cream

1   Put the milk, yoghurt and sauce into a blender and work them into a frothy liquid.
2   Pour the shake into a tall glass and top with the ice cream.

• WHITE CHOCOLATE • MILKSHAKE WITH CHOCOLATE FLAKE

Serves 1 (or 2 small children)

25 g/1 oz white chocolate
100 ml/4 fl oz/½ cup whipping cream
100 ml/4 fl oz/½ cup milk
1 chocolate flake (halved for small children)

1   Mix together the whipping cream and the milk, reserving 45 ml/3 tbsp of the milk.
2   Melt the white chocolate in the top of a double boiler with the reserved milk mixture.
3   Pour the white chocolate mixture into a blender. Add the remaining milk mixture and blend until well mixed. Chill.
4   Blend again. Pour into a glass and serve with a chocolate flake for older children; 2 glasses each decorated with half a flake for the younger ones.

• APRICOT ICE CREAM •

(suitable for diabetics)
Serves 6

425 g/15 oz jar/1⅓ cups apricot jam (diabetic)
450 ml/15 fl oz/2 cups plain low-fat yoghurt

1   Mix together the jam and the yoghurt until smooth.
2   Pour into a container and freeze, beating several times during freezing.

• BLACKCURRANT OR • BLUEBERRY ICE CREAM

450 g/1 lb frozen or canned blackcurrants or blueberries
2 large eggs
pinch of salt
175 g/6 oz/¾ cup caster sugar
5 tbsp water
300 ml/½ pt/1¼ cups double cream, whipped

1   Purée the fruit in a blender or food processor, having first drained off any juice.
2   Beat the eggs and salt together until frothy.
3   Place the sugar and water in a pan and

heat gently until dissolved, then boil for 3 minutes. Do not stir the syrup.
4   Pour in a steady stream on to the eggs, beating until thickened. Beat in the fruit purée, then fold in the cream.

• CHOCOLATE • ICE CREAM

Makes approx. 1.5 litres/ 2½ pints/6 cups

400 ml/14 fl oz/1¾ cups condensed milk
3 medium-sized eggs
1 tbsp cocoa powder blended with 2 tbsp warm water
300 ml/½ pt/1¼ cups double cream – whipped

1   Beat the condensed milk and eggs together in a heatproof bowl or mixer, then stir in the blended cocoa.
2   Place over a medium heat and stir constantly until thick enough to coat the back of the spoon. Remove from the heat and leave to cool. Fold in the cream.
3   Pour into a rigid freezer-proof container, cover, seal and freeze for 1 hour. Stir well, then re-freeze for 1 hour. Stir well, then re-freeze until firm.

• FROZEN • BANANA LOLLIES

Makes 6

3 firm bananas
100 g/4 oz/½ cup low-fat natural yoghurt
75 g/3 oz/¾ cup chopped mixed nuts

1   Peel and cut the bananas in half across. Spear each cut end with an ice cream stick and freeze.
2   When frozen, roll each banana lolly in the yoghurt, followed by chopped nuts.
3   Return to the freezer and freeze until solid. Remove from freezer 5 minutes before eating.

• HONEY YOGHURT ICE •

Serves 6

750 ml/25 fl oz/3 cups plain low-fat yoghurt
90 ml/6 tbsp strongly perfumed runny honey

1   Stir the honey into the yoghurt, adding more honey if not sweet enough.
2   Pour into a container and freeze, beating several times during freezing.

• MINT ICE CREAM •

2½ tbsp custard powder
300 ml/½ pt/1¼ cups milk
175 ml/6 fl oz/¾ cup evaporated milk
2 medium-sized eggs, separated
3–3½ tbsp icing sugar
25 g/1 oz/2 tbsp butter
1 tsp peppermint syrup or peppermint flavouring
few drops green food colouring

1   Beat the custard powder with 2 tablespoons milk in an electric mixer.
2   Heat the remaining milk and evaporated milk until boiling and stir into the mixture. Return to the pan and heat, stirring, until very thick.
3   Return to the bowl and beat in the egg yolks gradually. Add icing sugar, butter, flavouring and colouring and beat in thoroughly.
4   Set aside until cold, beating occasionally.
5   Beat egg whites until stiff and fold into the cold custard. Transfer to a freezer-proof container. Cover and freeze.

• RASPBERRY • ICE CREAM

Ingredients as Strawberry ice cream except use 175 g/6 oz/1 cup raspberries puréed in an electric blender or food processor to make 300 ml/ ½ pt/¾ cup purée

Proceed as above but stir in raspberry purée.

• RASPBERRY • ICE CREAM

Serves 6

450 g/1 lb fresh frozen raspberries
225 g/8 oz caster sugar
600 ml/1 pt/2½ cups whipping cream

1   Rub the berries, thawed if frozen, through a sieve. Add the sugar and stir until the sugar is dissolved.
2   Whip the cream until it holds soft

peaks. Combine with the sweetened purée and beat lightly together.

3 Pour into a container and freeze, beating vigorously at least once while partially frozen.

● RICH ●
VANILLA ICE CREAM

Serves 6

300 ml/10 fl oz/1¼ cups clotted cream
170 g/6 oz can/¾ cup sweetened
condensed milk, well chilled
5 ml/1 tsp vanilla essence

1 Put clotted cream and condensed milk into a bowl, add the vanilla essence and beat until they are well blended.

2 Turn into a shallow tray, such as an ice tray, and freeze without stirring until firm.

Note
Remove only 5 minutes before serving as its melts very quickly.

● STRAWBERRY ●
ICE CREAM

4 medium-size eggs, separated
125 g/4 oz/1 cup icing sugar, sifted
11 oz double cream
175 g/6 oz/1 cup strawberries puréed in
an electric blender or food processor to
make about 150 ml/¼ pt/⅔ cup purée

1 Beat the egg yolks until blended. Beat the egg whites until they stand in soft peaks, then beat in the icing sugar a tablespoon at a time until stiff.

2 Whip the cream until it stands in soft peaks, then fold into the egg white mixture with the yolks. Stir in the strawberry purée.

3 Turn into a 1.8 litre/2¾ pint/7 cups container and freeze.

● VANILLA ICE CREAM ●

Serves 6

600 ml/20 fl oz/2¼ cups whipping cream
50 g/2 oz/4 tbsp caster sugar
10 ml/2 tsp vanilla essence

1 Lightly whip cream and vanilla essence until soft peaks are formed. Fold in caster sugar.

2 Spoon into a container and freeze, beating lightly 2 or 3 times while freezing.

● BUTTER ICING ●

100 g/4 oz/½ cup butter, softened
225 g/8 oz/1 cup icing sugar
1–2 tbsp liquid: water, fruit juice or essence

Sieve icing sugar. Beat the butter until creamy then add the icing sugar bit by bit, beating well after each addition. Carefully mix in liquid.

● CHOCOLATE ●
COATING ICING

50 g/2 oz/4 tbsp butter
60 ml/4 tbsp golden syrup
60 ml/4 tbsp cocoa powder
60 ml/4 tbsp sifted icing sugar

1 Melt together butter and syrup. Stir in the cocoa and icing sugar and beat well until smooth.

2 Pour over the cooled cake.

● CHOCOLATE ●
FUDGE ICING

15 ml/1 tbsp cocoa powder
225 g/8 oz/2 cups icing sugar
50 g/2 oz/4 tbsp butter
15 ml/1 tbsp milk
30 ml/2 tbsp hot water

1 Sift the icing sugar and cocoa powder into a bowl.

2 Gently melt the butter in a small pan with milk and water. Bring just to the boil and then immediately pour on to the sieved cocoa and sugar. Stir with a wooden spoon.

3 Continue stirring until thick enough to spread.

4 Cover the cake and leave to set for about 1 hour.

● CHOCOLATE ICING ●

100 g/4 oz/½ cup plain chocolate or
chocolate drops
100 ml/4 tbsp water
100 g/4 oz/1 cup icing sugar, sifted

1 Break the chocolate into pieces and place with water in a bowl over a pan of hot water. Melt together and stir well. Gradually stir in the icing sugar until smooth.

2 Stand the cake on a wire rack. Pour the icing on to the centre of the cake and gently coax it over the sides, spreading it smoothly with a palette knife. Leave the icing to set.

● ROYAL ICING ●

2–3 egg whites
450 g/1 lb/4 cups icing sugar

Add the beaten egg whites bit by bit to the sugar, beating thoroughly all the time. Continue beating until the icing is smooth and white.

● SUGAR-FREE ●
FROSTING

125 g/4 oz/½ cup cream cheese
15 ml/1 tbsp cream
5 ml/1 tsp vanilla essence
1.25 ml/¼ tsp salt
liquid artificial sweetener to taste
zest of one orange

Blend all the ingredients together and sweeten to taste. Only put on the cake a few hours ahead or the cream cheese will crack.

● SUGAR PASTE ●

You can now buy ready made sugar paste in many supermarkets (called Regal ice or sometimes modelling icing) but if you want to make your own it's not difficult. You will find liquid glucose in specialist cookery shops or chemists.

450 g/1 lb/4 cups sieved icing sugar
1 egg white
2 oz liquid glucose

Warm the glucose until it is slightly runny,

then mix all ingredients together. Knead well until it becomes a smooth paste. Always keep it in a plastic bag or wrapped in clingfilm in the fridge while not using it.

• BOLOGNESE SAUCE •

For 6 portions

1 onion
1 carrot
1 stick celery
½ beef stock cube
15 ml/1 tbsp vegetable oil
225 g/8 oz beef mince
225 g/8 oz can/1 cup peeled tomatoes
30 ml/2 tbsp tomato purée
5 ml/1 tsp sugar
salt and pepper

1   Chop onion, carrot and celery finely. Melt oil and sauté until soft but not brown. Add mince and stir until lightly browned. Add tomatoes, tomato purée, stock cube, sugar and salt and pepper.
2   Cook gently for about 40 minutes, stirring occasionally.

• BROWN RICE •

Serves 6 young children

100 g/4 oz/²⁄₃ cup brown rice
15 g/½ oz/1 tbsp butter

1   Cook the rice in plenty of boiling salted water for 25 minutes. Drain.
2   Put the drained rice back in the saucepan with the butter, cover and leave for 5 minutes.

Note
Allow 50 g/2 oz/⅓ cup of rice per adult.

• CANNELLONI •

Serves 6 or 12

FOR VEGETARIANS
12 cannelloni, cooked according to packet instructions
250 g/8.8 oz/³⁄₄ cup frozen chopped spinach
salt to taste
1 onion, finely chopped
200 g/7 oz/1 cup cottage cheese
25 g/1 oz/2 tbsp butter
1 egg yolk
75 g/3 oz/⅓ cup grated Cheddar cheese
2 quantities of Tomato Sauce (page 111)

1   Pre-heat oven to 200°C/400°F/ gas 6.
2   Cook frozen spinach according to packet instructions. Drain.
3   Sauté onion in the butter until pale gold. Add spinach and sauté for 2 to 3 minutes. Transfer to a mixing bowl.
4   Add cottage cheese, egg yolk and salt to taste. Mix ingredients together with a fork.
5   Stuff the pre-cooked cannelloni with the mixture and place one or two in individual lightly buttered dishes. Cover with tomato sauce and sprinkle with grated cheese.
6   Cook for 15 minutes in the centre of the oven until the cheese is bubbly and brown.

FOR NON-VEGETARIANS
Fill with 1 recipe of Bolognese Sauce.

Note
If using 'no-cook cannelloni' follow cooking temperature and times on the packet.

• CHICKEN • WITH GRAPES

Serves 6

6 chicken breasts, skinned and fat removed
2 carrots, peeled and sliced
1 leek, peeled and sliced
600 ml/1 pt/2½ cups chicken stock (made with stock cube)
30 ml/2 tbsp parsley, chopped
salt and freshly ground black pepper
175 g/6 oz/²⁄₃ cup seedless grapes
25 g/1 oz/2 tbsp butter
1 onion, finely chopped
25 g/1 oz/3 tbsp plain flour
juice of 1 lemon
60 ml/4 tbsp double cream

1   Put carrots and leek in a saucepan. Add stock, parsley and seasoning. Cover and simmer for 25 minutes.
2   Plunge grapes into boiling water for about 10 seconds, drain, cool and skin them.
3   Strain and reserve the stock. Discard the vegetables.
4   Melt the butter in a saucepan and sauté the onion until soft but not coloured. Stir in the flour and cook over a low heat for 2 minutes. Gradually add the stock to the pan to make a thick, smooth sauce, stirring constantly. Simmer for 20 minutes.

Remove from the heat, add half the lemon juice and the cream. Cover and leave until ready to serve.
5   Pre-heat the oven to 180°C/350°F/ gas 4. Sprinkle the chicken breasts with the remaining lemon juice, season with salt and pepper, cover with foil and cook for 25 minutes.
6   Reheat the sauce and toss in the grapes at the last moment. Place the chicken breasts on a serving dish and coat with the sauce.

• CHICKEN NUGGETS •

16 to 18 nuggets

2 chicken breast fillets
25 g/1 oz/3 tbsp wholemeal flour
salt and pepper
1 medium-sized egg
50 g/2 oz/½ cup breadcrumbs made from wholemeal bread

1   Pre-heat oven to 200°C/400°F/ gas 6.
2   Remove any fat and white tendons from chicken breasts and cut each into 8 or 9 chunks.
3   Sift flour, salt and pepper and toss chicken chunks in this until well coated.
4   Beat egg in a bowl. Put breadcrumbs on a plate. Then turn chicken chunks first in the beaten egg and then in the bread-crumbs. Place on a lightly greased baking sheet or roasting tin.
5   Bake for 15 minutes in the centre of the oven. Serve hot or cold.

Note
These may be prepared, frozen, and cooked from frozen in an oven pre-heated to 200°C/400°F/gas 6 for 25 minutes.

• CRUNCHY FISH •

18 pieces

350 g/³⁄₄ lb cold fillet
50 g/2 oz/1 cup plain flour
salt and pepper
1 medium-sized egg, beaten
25 g/1 oz/1 cup cornflakes, crushed
50 g/2 oz/¼ cup Cheddar cheese, finely grated

1   Pre-heat the oven to 200°C/400°F/ gas mark 6.
2   Cut the fish into 18 pieces. Place the seasoned flour and beaten egg in two

separate bowls. Mix the crushed cornflakes and grated cheese in a third bowl. Coat a few pieces of the fish with the flour, dip in the beaten egg and coat with the cheese mixture. Transfer to a baking sheet. Repeat with the remaining fish pieces.
3   Cook in the centre of the oven for 10 to 15 minutes. Serve hot.

• HAMBURGERS •

175–225 g/6–8 oz sirloin or rump steak
per person
15 ml/1 tbsp butter
15 ml/1 tbsp oil
salt and freshly ground black pepper

1   Trim any fat from the meat, cut the meat into pieces. Mince the meat through coarse blade of the mincer. Shape into a round 4 cm/1½ in thick. Younger children may prefer half-size hamburgers. Do not overhandle as this will toughen the meat. Leave it to rest.
2   Heat the butter and oil in the frying pan. Fry the burger for 3 minutes on each side for medium rare, and 4 minutes on each side for medium. Season with salt and pepper.

Note
This can be made in a food processor, but the texture will not be quite the same.

• HOME-MADE BAKED BEANS •

Serves 12

450 g/1 lb/2½ cups white kidney beans
2 yellow onions, finely chopped
40 g/1½ oz/3 tbsp butter
25 g/1 oz/3 tbsp flour
75 ml/5 tbsp tomato ketchup
30 ml/2 tbsp tomato purée
15 ml/1 tbsp demerara sugar
salt and freshly ground black pepper

1   Soak the beans in water overnight. Drain the beans. Bring to the boil in fresh water and simmer for one hour. Drain the beans, reserving 600 ml/ 1 pt/2½ cups of the liquid.
2   In a casserole, melt the butter and sauté the finely chopped onions until soft and golden. Add the flour and cook gently for 4 minutes. Add the bean water, bring to the boil, stirring constantly until thickened.

Reduce to a simmer and cook for 5 minutes. Add the tomato ketchup, tomato purée, demerara sugar and season to taste with black pepper. Add the cooked beans.
3   Cover and simmer for 30 minutes or until the beans are soft. Season with salt.

• LAMB BURGERS •

1.4 kg/3 lb breast of lamb
(700 g/1½ lb trimmed weight)
salt and freshly ground black pepper
flour
oil
600 ml/1 pint/2½ cups hot chicken stock

1   Mince or finely chop the breast of lamb. Season the meat with salt and freshly ground black pepper. Form the lamb into 12 balls, rolling them in your hands until smooth.
2   Heat the oven to 180°C/350°F/gas 4. Coat the lamb balls in the flour, and brown them in the oil. Place in a casserole with the hot stock and cook, covered, for 30 to 40 minutes in the oven.

• MACARONI CHEESE •

Serves 6

225 g/8 oz macaroni
25 g/1 oz/2 tbsp butter
25 g/1 oz/3 tbsp plain flour
600 ml/1 pt/2½ cups milk
salt and pepper
175 g/6 oz/¾ cup grated Cheddar cheese
30 ml/2 tbsp fresh wholemeal
breadcrumbs
25 g/1 oz/2 tbsp melted butter

1   Pre-heat oven to 200°C/400°F/ gas 6.
2   Cook the macaroni, uncovered, in plenty of boiling salted water for about 15 minutes. Drain.
3   Meanwhile melt 25 g/1 oz/2 tbsp butter in a pan, add the flour and stir for 2–3 minutes. Gradually add the milk, stirring continuously, until the mixture thickens. Cook slowly for 5 minutes. Stir in 100 g/4 oz/½ cup of the grated cheese.
4   Fold the macaroni into the sauce the spoon the mixture into a buttered oven-proof dish.
5   Mix the remaining cheese with the breadcrumbs, sprinkle over the macaroni and pour the melted butter over the top.
6   Bake for 20 minutes or until the top is golden and crisp.

Note
This dish can also be prepared in individual ramekins.
It can be made in advance as far as paragraph 5 and refrigerated until ready to cook.

• MINI SHEPHERD'S PIES •

6 portions

30 ml/2 tbsp vegetable oil
2 onions, finely chopped
450 g/1 lb minced beef or lamb
25 g/1 oz/3 tbsp flour
125 ml/¼ pt/⅔ cup beef stock or gravy
20 ml/2 tbsp tomato purée
30 ml/2 tbsp tomato ketchup
1.25 ml/¼ tsp Worcestershire sauce
salt and black pepper
30–45 ml/2–3 tbsp milk
450 g/1 lb/2 cups potatoes, mashed

1   Pre-heat the oven to 180°C/350°F/ gas mark 4.
2   Cook the onions in the oil until soft. Add the meat and cook until lightly browned, then add the flour and cook for 2 to 3 minutes.
3   Stir in the stock, tomato purée, ketchup, Worcestershire sauce and seasoning. Cook gently, covered, for 10 minutes, stirring occasionally.
4   Heat the butter and the milk and beat into the mashed potatoes.
5   Divide meat mixture between 6 greased ramekin dishes. Cover with mashed potatoes and ripple the top with a fork.
6   Bake near the top of the oven for 30 minutes or until brown.

Note
These can be made in advance and refrigerated until you are ready to cook them.

• MINI • TOAD-IN-THE-HOLE

Serves 12

lard, dripping or solid vegetable fat
24 'cocktail' sausages
1 recipe Yorkshire pudding batter

1   Pre-heat the oven to 220°C/425°F/ gas mark 7.
2   Grease 12 individual Yorkshire pudding tins with 2 tbsp of dripping or lard. Place 2 sausages in each tin and bake

in the oven for 10 minutes or until sizzling.
3   Remove from the oven and fill each tin
²⁄₃ full of Yorkshire pudding batter.
4   Cook in the top of the oven for about
20 minutes or until well risen and crisp.
5   Serve at once.

• OVEN-BARBECUED •
SPARE RIBS

Serves 6

12 pork spare ribs
20 ml/4 tbsp clear honey
45 ml/4 tbsp soy sauce
60 ml/4 tbsp tomato ketchup
black pepper
15 ml/1 tbsp wine vinegar

1   Pre-heat oven to 180°C/350°F/ gas 4.
2   Grill ribs for 10 to 15 minutes under a
high grill until brown, turning them
occasionally.
3   Arrange ribs in a single layer in a large
roasting tin and pour over the pan juices.
4   Mix together honey, soy sauce, tomato
ketchup. Season with black pepper, then
add vinegar. Pour over spare ribs.
5   Cook, uncovered, in the centre of the
oven for 30 minutes.

Note
The spare ribs can be grilled and
marinated in the honey mixture in the
refrigerator until you are ready to cook
them.

• PANCAKES •

Makes 8 to 10 pancakes

100 g/4 oz/1 cup plain flour
pinch of salt
1 egg, lightly beaten
300 ml/10 fl oz/1¼ cups milk
vegetable oil for greasing

1   Sift the flour and salt into a large bowl.
Using a wooden spoon, make a hollow in
the centre of the flour and pour in the
lightly beaten egg. Slowly pour half the
milk into the flour, gradually working the
flour into the milk. When all the flour is
incorporated, beat the mixture until it
becomes smooth and free of lumps. Allow
to rest for a few minutes then add the
remainder of the milk, beating continuously until the mixture has the consistency of single cream.

2   Using an 18 cm/7 in heavy-based
frying pan heat just enough fat to gloss the
bottom of the pan. Pour in just enough
batter to coat the bottom of the pan, tilting
the pan to spread it. The underside of the
pancake should be golden in one minute.
Turn the pancake with a palette knife or
spatula and cook for a further minute.
3   Stack the pancakes in a pile with a piece
of greaseproof paper between each pancake until ready to use.

Note
These can be frozen.

• PIZZA DOUGH •

225 g/8 oz/2 cups plain flour
2.5 ml/½ tsp salt
50 ml/2 fl oz/4 tbsp milk
5 ml/1 tsp caster sugar
25 g/1 oz/2 tbsp butter, melted
1 medium-sized egg, beaten

1   Sift the flour and salt into a bowl.
2   Heat the milk until tepid; cream one
tablespoon of the milk with the sugar and
yeast.
3   Make a well in the centre of the flour.
Pour in the yeast, milk, melted butter and
beaten egg into the centre. Mix and work
the dough until it leaves the side of the
bowl clean. Form the dough into a smooth
ball and leave it in the bowl, covered with a
cloth, or in an oiled polythene bag, in a
warm place until twice its size.
4   When the dough has risen, heat the oil
to 220°C/425°F/gas 7. Knead the dough
lightly for 1 to 2 minutes. Roll in into a
30 cm/12 in circle and place it on a greased
and floured baking tray. Cover the dough
with the filling of your choice. Bake in the
preheated oven for 20 to 25 minutes, or
until the dough has risen well.

Note
This dough could be made in a food
processor, but be very careful not to
overprocess as it will make the dough very
elastic. Use short, sharp bursts.

• SALMON MOUSSE •

450 g/1 lb fresh salmon
300 ml/½ pt/1¼ cups milk
1 bay leaf
1 small onion
25 g/1 oz/2 tbsp butter
25 g/1 oz/3 tbsp plain flour
salt
freshly ground pepper
150 ml/¼ pt/²⁄₃ cup mayonnaise
1 sachet gelatine dissolved in
3 tbsp of water
150 ml/¼ pt/²⁄₃ cup double cream

1   Butter a square of foil and encase
salmon in it, wrapping like a parcel.
2   Place in a saucepan and cover with cold
water. Bring to the boil over a gentle heat.
3   Simmer for 10 minutes, drain and
allow to cool.
4   When cool, unwrap, remove skin and
all bones from the salmon and set aside.
5   Measure milk into a saucepan with bay
leaf and peeled onion.
6   Bring slowly to the boil. Draw off the
heat and leave to infuse.
7   Strain milk and reserve.
8   Melt butter in a saucepan and stir in
the flour.
9   Cook gently for 1 minute, then stir in
the milk beating well to obtain a smooth
sauce.
10   Season with salt and pepper.
11   Cover the surface of the sauce with a
piece of buttered paper.
12   Beat the salmon until smooth, beat in
the sauce and mayonnaise.
13   Dissolve the gelatine in water over
gentle heat. Allow to cool.
14   Pour in a steady stream on to the
salmon mixture, beating all the time.
15   Lightly whip the cream and fold into
the mixture.
16   Pour into individual fish moulds or
ramekins.
17   Chill until ready to serve.
18   Unmould onto plates.

• SAUSAGE •
SAILING BOATS

Serves 6

6 pork or beef sausages, each about
10 cm/4 in long
1½ tomatoes, cut into quarters
6 cocktail sticks
700 g/1½ lb potatoes
30 ml/2tbsp milk
few drops blue food colouring
25 g/1 oz/2 tbsp butter
salt and pepper

1   Pre-heat the oven to 190°C/375°F/ gas mark 5.
2   Prick sausages with a fork and place in a roasting tin. Cook for 30 minutes or until they are crisp and brown.
3   Meanwhile peel and wash the potatoes and cut into pieces. Simmer in salted water for about 20 minutes or until cooked. Drain and mash with milk, a few drops of blue food colouring, butter, salt and pepper. Place the mashed potato on an oval dish and fork into waves.
4   Put a cocktail stick through the length of each piece of tomato and stick one into each sausage so that it looks like a sail.
5   Place the sausage boats on the mashed potato and serve immediately.

• SMOKY BACON •
DRUMSTICKS

Serves 6

6 chicken drumsticks, with skin removed
75 g/3 oz/3 cups smoky bacon-flavoured
potato crisps
75 g/3 oz/⅓ cup mature Cheddar
cheese, finely grated
1 medium-sized egg

1   Pre-heat the oven to 180°C/350°F/ gas 4.
2   Crush the potato crisps and mix with the grated cheese.
3   Beat the egg and dip each drumstick into the beaten egg. Press on crisp mixture to each drumstick.
4   Place the coated drumsticks on a greased baking tray and sprinkle with any remaining crisp mixture.
5   Bake uncovered for 40 to 50 minutes. May be served hot or cold.

Note
These can be prepared and frozen, but they must be completely defrosted before

they are cooked. Alternatively they can be pre-cooked for 30 minutes, cooled and chilled. When ready to serve cook them for a further 15 to 20 minutes.

• VEGETARIAN MINI •
YORKSHIRE PUDDINGS

Makes 12

100 g/4 oz/1 cup plain flour
pinch of salt
2 medium-sized eggs
125 ml/¼ pt/⅔ cup milk
solid vegetable fat
180/ml/12 tbsp tomato ketchup
75 g/3 oz/⅓ cup Cheddar cheese, grated

1   Sift the flour and salt into a large bowl. Make a hollow in the centre and pour in the lightly beaten eggs. Slowly pour the milk into the flour, gradually working the flour into the milk. When all the flour is incorporated beat the mixture with a wooden spoon until it has the consistency of single cream. Leave the mixture to stand for 15 minutes.
2   When ready to cook heat the oven to 220°C/425°F/gas 7.
3   Grease 12 individual Yorkshire pudding tins with small knobs of vegetable fat and heat in the oven until the fat is smoking hot. Remove from the oven and pour the batter into the tins so that they are each about ⅔ full.
4   Cook in the top of the oven for about 20 minutes or until well risen and crisp.
5   Fill each with 15 ml/1 tbsp tomato ketchup and top with grated cheese. Reduce the oven temperature to 180°C/ 350°F/gas 4 and cook for a further 5 minutes until the cheese has melted.

Note
The Yorkshire puddings may be made in the food processor.
They may be frozen. When you remove them from the deep freeze, fill with ketchup and cheese and cook them at 180°C/350°F/gas 4 for 15 minutes.

• CHOCOLATE MOUSSE •

Serves 6

225 g/8 oz plain chocolate or
chocolate drops
15 g/½ oz/1 tbsp butter
3 medium-sized eggs, separated
15 ml/1 tbsp coffee essence (optional)

1   Put the chocolate, broken into small pieces, and the butter in a bowl placed over a pan of hot, not boiling, water, Leave to melt, stirring occasionally.
2   When the chocolate is completely melted remove it from the heat and beat in the egg yolks and coffee essence (if desired). Beat the egg whites until they form stiff peaks and fold them into the mixture.
3   Pour into 6 individual glasses and leave in a cool place until set.

Note
These can be decorated with grated chocolate or chocolate curls just before serving.

• EXOTIC FRUIT SALAD •

Serves 6

45 ml/3 tbsp sugar
juice of 1 lemon
1 large mango
2 passion fruit
2 kiwi fruit
2 nectarines
2 bananas

1   Mix the sugar and lemon in a large bowl until dissolved.
2   Add mango (peeled and diced), passion fruit (cut in half and flesh scooped out), kiwi fruit (peeled and sliced), nectarines (stoned and sliced) and bananas (sliced). Mix well.

Note
If making this in advance add the sliced bananas at the last moment to prevent them discolouring.

• FRUIT JUICE JELLY •

Serves 6

450 ml/¾ pt/2 cups orange juice from a
carton
1 sachet gelatine

1   Soak the gelatine in 45 ml/3 tbsp orange juice for 5 minutes.
2   Pour remainder of juice into a pan and heat to just below boiling point. Add to the gelatine mixture and stir vigorously until dissolved.
3   Cool, then pour into a dampened mould. Refrigerate until completely set – approximately 3 hours.

4 Turn out of mould by dipping the mould into hot water for 10 seconds.

Note
Only heat the fruit juice until hot enough to dissolve the gelatine. Do not boil or you will destroy the taste of the fruit.

• PINK MILKSHAKE • JELLY

Serves 6 to 10

1 small packet raspberry or strawberry jelly
150 ml/5 fl oz/²⁄₃ cup warm water
150 ml/5 fl oz/²⁄₃ cup cold water
175 ml/6 fl oz/³⁄₄ cup evaporated milk, chilled

1 Dissolve the jelly in the warm water, then stir in the cold water.
2 Chill the jelly in the refrigerator until on the point of setting. This will take 1 to 1¼ hours.
3 In a large bowl beat the evaporated milk until it is thick and frothy. Gradually beat in the thickened jelly.
4 Put the mixture into a dampened jelly mould or into individual glasses. Return to refrigerator to set.

Note
Chill the jelly in a flat container so that the jelly sets evenly.

• ST CLEMENTS • APPLE SNOW

Serves 6

700 g/1½ lbs cooking apples
finely grated zest and juice of 1 large orange
finely grated zest and juice of 1 large lemon
3 medium-sized egg whites
100 g/4 oz/½ cup caster sugar

1 Peel, core and slice the apples.
2 Put them in a pan with the juice of the orange and lemon and simmer gently until the apple is pulpy.
3 Sieve the apple mixture, or purée in a blender or food processor until smooth. Leave to cool.
4 2 hours before the meal, beat the egg whites until stiff, then beat in the sugar. Fold the egg white into the apple purée.

• SMOKED • SALMON PÂTÉ

Serves 6

100 g/4 oz/²⁄₃ cup smoked salmon pieces
100 g/4 oz/½ cup cream cheese
pepper
juice of ½ lemon

1 Blend the salmon, cream cheese and lemon juice in a food processor until smooth. Season with pepper.
2 Serve with brown bread, thinly sliced and buttered, and wedges of lemon.

• TOMATO SAUCE •

30/ml/2 tbsp vegetable oil
1 onion, finely chopped
425 g/15 oz can/2 cups peeled Italian tomatoes
15 ml/1 tbsp tomato purée/paste
5 ml/1 tsp sugar
salt and freshly ground black pepper

In a saucepan heat the oil and cook the finely chopped onion until softened. Add the remaining ingredients and simmer, covered, for 20 minutes.

COSTUME INSTRUCTIONS

Note: All measurements are actual and you should add 12mm/½in for your seams.

• ANIMAL HEADS •

fur remnants for bear, rabbit, cat
felt piece for mouse
elastic

Head shape is the same for each animal. Cut as shown and sew each side piece to centre along A–B. Elasticate around back of head from ear to ear.

Choose your ears and cut out 4 shapes (diagram). Right sides together stitch each pair together along upper edge then turn inside out. Pinch a pleat in the centre lower edge of each ear and stitch onto head piece.

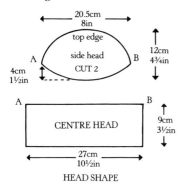

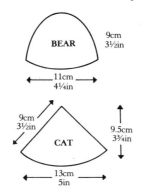

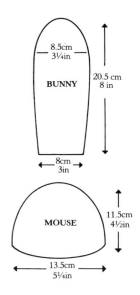

• BATMAN •

grey tights
grey leotard or .5 m/20 in grey jersey
1.5 m/5 ft dark blue jersey
yellow and black felt
Wonderweb
velcro
narrow elastic

Make shorts, boots and gauntlets as for Superman, in dark blue jersey. Make cloak also, as above, but cutting hem as shown.

Shirt Top

If you cannot find a leotard, use grey jersey to make top. Cut as diagram. Sew shoulder seams, then sleeve heads to armholes. Join underarm seams and side seams all in one. Hem neck, wrist and bottom edges.

Logo

Cut out bat and background and make as for Superman. Apply to chest.

Belt

Cut in blue jersey, 5 cm/2 in wide, to fit waist, adding on 2.5 cm/1 in overlap for velcro fastening. Back with black felt for strength. Sew on strips of yellow felt as for Superman.

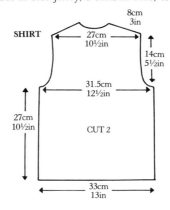

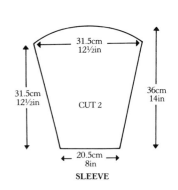

Hood

Cut as diagram, in dark blue. Sew together back seam and side seams going around ears and over top of head. Fit on head to mark eyes. Remove and cut eyeholes.

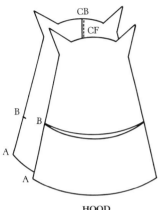

HOOD

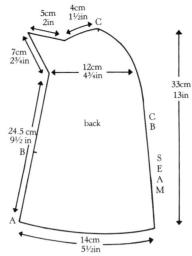

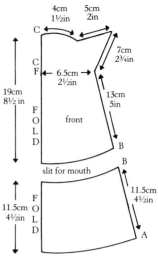

slit for mouth

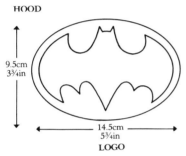

LOGO

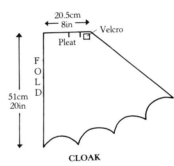

CLOAK

• CHRISTMAS TREE •

2 m/78 in green fabric
green crepe paper (2 packs)
decorations
green card or white card and green spray
elastic

Body

Cut shapes as shown. Sew up shoulders and side seams. Gather on strips of crepe paper, using wider widths at bottom. Sew

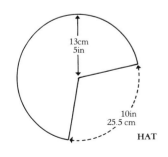

HAT

FRONT BODY SHAPE

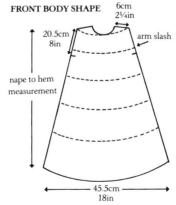

up back seam leaving top 15 cm/6 in open for access. Attach ties.

Hat

Cut shape in card as shown. Spray green. Gather narrow strips of crepe paper

BACK BODY SHAPE

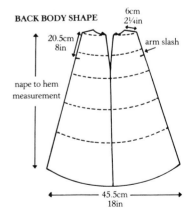

around. Staple edges together. Staple elastic on to fit under chin.
   Decorate.

• DISCO SKIRT •

1.1 m/44 in black satin
(114 cm/46 in wide)
1.1 m/44 in pink net
2.5 cm/1 in wide elastic

Following diagram, cut a half circle in black satin and same of net. Join each piece to complete the half circle. Cut 4 strips of satin, and 4 of net, each 15 cm/6 in wide. Join satin strips end to end and gather up to fit lower edge of skirt. Sew on. Do same with the net. Cut elastic to fit child's waist and sew ends together. Gather waist edge of satin skirt and attach along upper edge of elastic with zig-zag stitch to allow stretching. Do same with net and sew on to elastic just below satin.

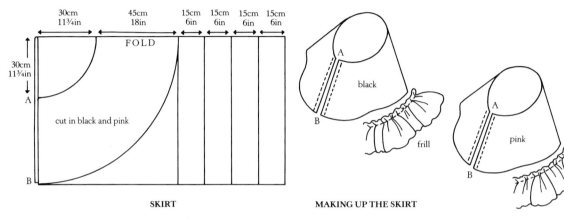

SKIRT   MAKING UP THE SKIRT

• DRACULA/DEVIL •

20 cm/8 in white jersey or white gloves
1.4 m/56 in black satin × 114 cm/45 in
1.4 m/56 in red satin × 114 cm/45 in
heavy iron-on vilene
6 black buttons
2.5 cm/1 in black elastic
velcro

Cloak

Cut as diagram, one shape in black, one in red. Right sides together, stitch together leaving neck edge open. Turn inside-out and press. Cut collar shape as shown, two in black, one in vilene. Iron interfacing to wrong side of one piece. Right sides together, stitch from A to B. Turn inside-out and press. Attach collar to neck edge of cloak.

Waistcoat

Cut waistcoat fronts as shown, two fronts in black, two in red. Cut black collar for black view of waistcoat. Right sides together, sew red to black pieces along edge from A to B and C to D. Turn inside-out and press. Stitch black collar to neck edges, to fall on black view of waistcoat front. Attach one piece of elastic from shoulder to shoulder fitting bend neck. Sew one piece of elastic to each side seam to fasten around back of waist with velcro. Overlap one side over the other and stitch buttons on both red and black sides, to join the waistcoat fronts. Sew velcro on at

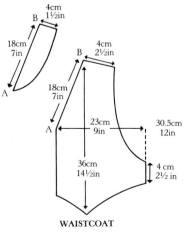

WAISTCOAT

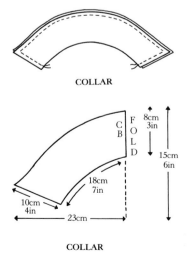

COLLAR

COLLAR

CLOAK

oulders for cloak to attach. Sew velcro on oak where shown.

or Dracula make white gloves as for uperman.

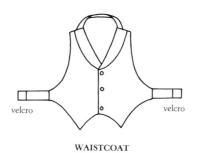

WAISTCOAT

For Devil we made a tail from 3 lengths red cord glued together, and a red card point glued to the end of it.

• ELIZABETH I •

m/78 in white muslin or old net curtaining
–3 curtains (or heavy fabric, brocade etc
115 cm/45 in wide)
50 cm/20 in stiff interfacing
90 cm/36 in wide
3 m/5 ft rigilene
gold coloured wood glue
white coloured wood glue
fruit gums
pasta wheels sprayed gold and silver
pasta bows sprayed gold
glass stones
pearl drops and strings of pearls
30 cm/12 in open ended zip
gold remnant or gold braid
stocking stuffed with newspaper
gold spray paint
vilene
shirring elastic

ut as fig. 1, one front and two backs from urtain or fabric, and one front from nterfacing. Stitch or iron interfacing to vrong side of front. Right sides together, titch front to backs at shoulder and side eams. Hem lower edge of bodice. On vrong side, stitch a length of rigilene down entre front of bodice and along lower ʹ-shaped edge. Finish off neck edge.

Sleeves
ut 2 shapes as fig. 2. Using gold braid or trips of gold remnant, decorate sleeves nd bodice in diagonal latticework. Stitch r glue in place. Pipe quatre-foil outlines in ach space with gold glue, and decorate vith white glue 'pearls' and fruit gum ewels in centres. Glue gold and silver wheel pasta along bottom edge and glue a lass stone or small boiled sweet in centre f each (fig. 3).

Tack a strip of white muslin or net down entre front, gather at invervals and glue old painted bow pasta over.

Right sides in, stitch underarm seam in each sleeve and, matching underarm seam with side seam of bodice, and centre sleeve with shoulder seam, gather both sleeves into armholes.

Stitch zip down centre back as instructions on packet.

Skirt
Use one curtain (in this case the reverse side) about 1.5 m/5 ft wide and 1.02 m/ 41 in deep. Spread on floor or table to decorate. With strips of white muslin/net about 7 cm/2¾ in wide, make a lattice work pattern, tacking and gathering at each intersection, and gluing on a pasta bow. Add gold and 'jewelled' quatre-foils in each space, as for sleeves. When all is dry, right sides together stitch up back seam. Gather up the rufflettes to fit waist, or make channel and thread with elastic.

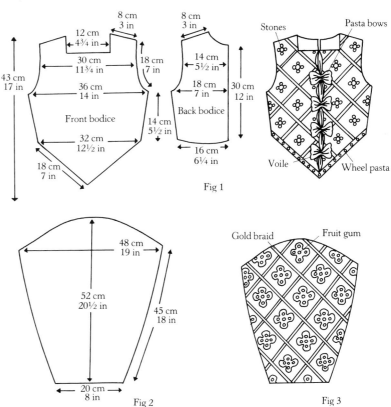

Fig 1
Fig 2
Fig 3

(To fit small child)
2.3 m/92 in white cheesecloth or old sheet
115 cm/46 in wide
50 cm/20 in white net 5 cm/2 in wide
black felt tip pen

Fold cheesecloth in half lengthwise and trim as necessary so that it will reach the ground when worn. With zig-zag stitch attach 4 layers of net to the front where face will be, then cut away cheesecloth. Make seams up sides, leaving openings for hands (fig. 1).

Cut strips of remaining net, slash and gather up (fig. 2).

● GHOST ●

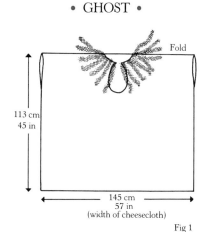

113 cm
45 in

Fold

145 cm
57 in
(width of cheesecloth)

Fig 1

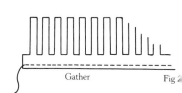

Gather

Fig 2

Stitch net hair to cheesecloth as shown in fig. 1.

Draw spooky face onto net with felt tip.

● HE-MAN ●

.5 m/20 in grey felt
.5 m/20 in red fur fabric
30 cm/1 ft red jersey
red felt
red Smarties
1.5 m/5 ft cord
Wonderweb
velcro
glue (UHU, Bostick gel)

Chest Piece

Cut rectangle as diagram. Straps are 4 cm/1½ in wide. Cut two 30.5 cm/1 ft long; two 46 cm/1.5 ft long, and one 15 cm/6 in long. Sew together as shown. Cut red cross and iron on to front with Wonderweb.

Boots

As for Superman, plus attach 2 strips of red jersey 2.5 cm/1 in wide on to each boot, on the sole edge at the instep. Use to lace up the leg. Also stitch 7.5 cm/3 in strip of fur around each boot top.

Shorts

Cut a front and back, as diagram, in red fur. Join at crotch, then proceed as for Superman.

SHORTS

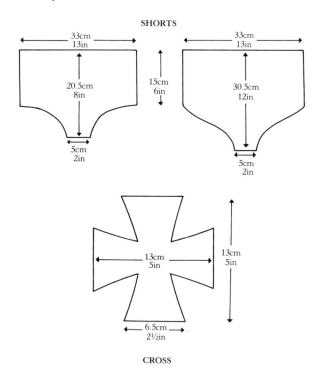

33cm
13in

20.5cm
8in

15cm
6in

33cm
13in

30.5cm
12in

5cm
2in

5cm
2in

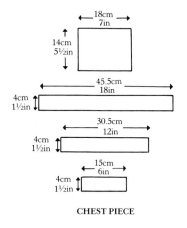

18cm
7in

14cm
5½in

45.5cm
18in

4cm
1½in

30.5cm
12in

4cm
1½in

15cm
6in

4cm
1½in

CHEST PIECE

13cm
5in

13cm
5in

6.5cm
2½in

CROSS

Belt

Make belt to fit child's waist, 4 cm/ 1½ in wide in red felt. Join with velcro. Glue red cord round edge, and glue red Smarties at intervals in centre.

Waistbands

Cut strips of fur 4 cm/1½ in wide to fit child's waist (and upper arm). Sew on velcro to join.

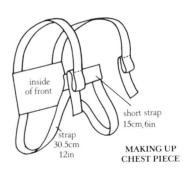

side view

top strap
back
sew through
front
bottom strap

inside of front
strap 30.5cm 12in
short strap 15cm, 6in

MAKING UP CHEST PIECE

• HENRY VIII •

3.5 m/140 in bright blue felt 90 cm/36 in wide
2.1 m/84 in pale blue felt 90 cm/36 in wide
2.3 m/92 in red velvet 90 cm/36 in wide (or old velvet curtain)
pasta circles painted gold, silver and jewel colours
gold braid, chains, and pearls
remnant of thin white cotton, voile etc
cotton wool or wadding
red satin remnant
blue feather
elastic
newspaper, old tights etc for stuffing

Cut 4 shapes as fig. 1 in pale blue felt.

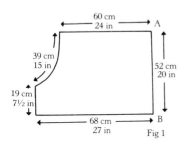

60 cm / 24 in → A
39 cm / 15 in
52 cm / 20 in
19 cm / 7½ in
68 cm / 27 in → B
Fig 1

Right sides together, stitch the two side seams A–B. Cut sixteen 52 cm/20 in lengths of bright blue felt 5.5 cm/2 in wide, and pin onto the right side of each of the pale blue pieces, at equal intervals, then stitch along waist and bottom edges (fig. 2).

Right side in, join inside leg seam on each piece. Matching both these seams stitch crutch seam (fig. 3).

Turn to inside 2 cm/1 in at waist and leg edges to form channel for elastic, leaving a gap for threading. Thread with elastic.

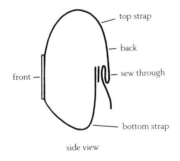

side seam
Fig 2

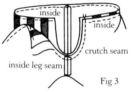

inside
inside
inside leg seam
crutch seam
Fig 3

Jacket

Cut 2 fronts and 1 back as fig. 4, in bright blue felt. Stitch fronts to back at shoulder and side seams.

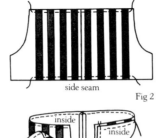

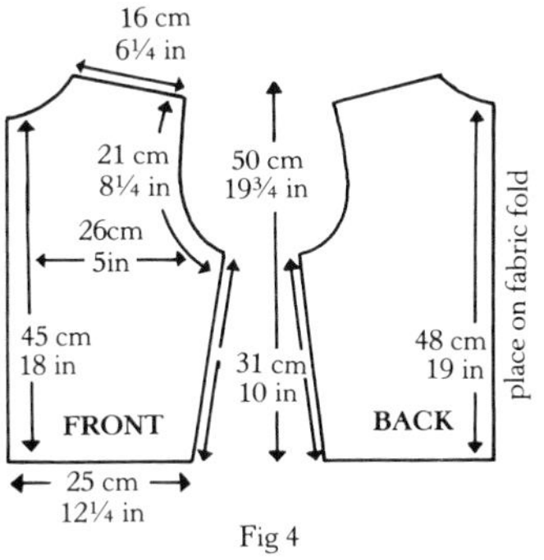

16 cm / 6¼ in
21 cm / 8¼ in
50 cm / 19¾ in
26cm / 5in
45 cm / 18 in
31 cm / 10 in
48 cm / 19 in
FRONT
BACK
place on fabric fold
25 cm / 12¼ in
Fig 4

Peplum

Cut 2 shapes in bright blue as fig. 5a and 2 as fig. 5b. Gather the lower edge of each front into the top edge of 5a, with corners A at centre front waist. Stitch both pieces 5b onto lower edge of back, with corners B at centre back.

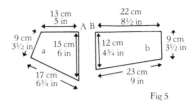

13 cm / 5 in
A B
22 cm / 8½ in
9 cm / 3½ in
15 cm / 6 in
a
12 cm / 4¾ in
b
9 cm / 3½ in
17 cm / 6¾ in
23 cm / 9 in
Fig 5

Sleeves

Cut 2 pieces of bright blue felt as fig. 6.

Make 5 vertical broken slashes in each piece, place a long strip of white thin fabric about 7 cm/2¾ in wide behind each slash line and pull a little through each slit, tacking into place. Between each white puff glue a piece of the painted pasta (fig. 7).

Slash the jacket front in the same way and pull more white fabric through. Decorate front edges with pasta. Right sides inside, sew underarm seams in both sleeves, turn right sides out and, matching underarm seams to jacket side seams, and centre top sleeves to shoulder seams, stitch both sleeves in.

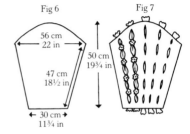

Fig 6
56 cm / 22 in
47 cm / 18½ in
30 cm / 11¾ in

Fig 7
50 cm / 19¾ in

Collar

Cut a 27 cm/10½ in length of bright blue felt 4 cm/1¾ in wide. Fit neck edge of jacket along one edge and stitch. Gather up 80 cm/32 in strips of white 5 cm/2 in wide and stitch behind cuff edges. Trim collar, cuffs, front edges and peplum with gold braid. Fasten with poppers.

Cape

Cut 1 back and 2 fronts as fig. 8 in red velvet. Make pleats in back neck edge to reduce measurement to 20 cm/7¾ in and machine in place. Right sides together, stitch fronts to back at shoulders and side seams as shown by dotted lines, leaving 32 cm/12½ in open for arms. Make pleats in each shoulder to reduce measurement to 9 cm/3½ in and stitch down. Finish edges.

Hat

Cut two circles of bright blue felt 36 cm/14 in diameter and stitch together round the edges. Cut a hole 16 cm/6¼ in diameter in the centre of one thickness. Turn hat right side out and decorate front with pasta, pearls and a feather.

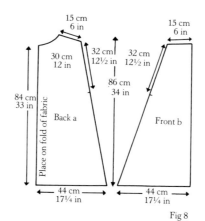

Fig 8

Shoes

Cut a right and a left sole in bright blue as fig. 9. Cut 2 front pieces in bright blue and 2 more in pale blue as fig. 9. Cut 3 slashes in bright blue as shown and pull bits of pale blue through the slits and tack in place.

Right sides together stitch the fronts over the soles around edges. Turn out and cut 2 strips of fabric 38 cm/15 in by 5 cm/2 in and stitch to the backs of the soles and to the sides of the front pieces. Stick or tack ties on, and stuff toes with wadding.

Make garter from long strip of slashed felt, gathered top and bottom.

Cut sash from red satin remnant fringed both ends.

Wear with suitable tights, and stuff tummy and pumpkin pants with wadding, newspapers, old tights etc.

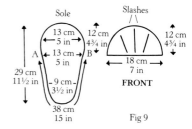

Fig 9

● HOLLY HEADDRESS ●

small quantity of green shiny lining fabric
6 small red Christmas tree balls
1 plastic headband
wire and fusewire

Cut 8 large holly leaves out of lining fabric and glue into pairs with wire in centre of each. Wind ends of wire around headband. Wind fusewire around balls and wire into position.

● LITTLE MISS MUFFET ●

I made this pretty dress from Little Vogue 1326 pattern. For the mob cap: cut a circle of white fabric, about 50 cm/20 in diameter. With shirring elastic in the bobbin of your machine, stitch four rows 10 cm/4 in in from the edge, to gather it up. Add a wooden bowl, spoon and rubber spider.

• MARY MARY •

70–80 cm/27½–31 in blue cotton
blue lavatory paper
shell pasta
silver paint
heavy vilene interfacing
elastic
small dolls

Dress

Cut as shown. Sew shoulder and side seams. Hem neck armholes and bottom edge. Sew lavatory paper on in tiers, gathering as you go. Then sew up back seam, leaving 15 cm/6 in open for head to go through. Attach ties. Sew similar frills around armholes. Cut petal shapes and sew round neck. Paint pasta silver and glue around neck. Use long strip of lavatory paper to tie around waist and make bow at back. Sew dolls on to front bodice.

Bonnet

Cut shape in vilene as for Sheera. Cut strips of lavatory paper 3 cm/1¼ in wide and gather in rows on one side of vilene, stitching down the centre. Cut blue cotton shape as shown, gather curved edge, and sew on to inside edge of vilene brim. Elasticate lower edge of cotton. Sew elastic on to corners of brim and fit under chin. Make bow of lavatory paper and sew on side.

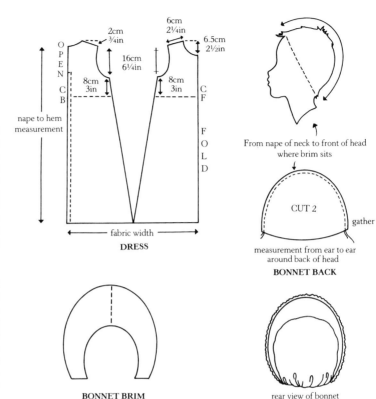

DRESS

From nape of neck to front of head where brim sits

BONNET BACK

measurement from ear to ear around back of head

BONNET BRIM

rear view of bonnet

• MR T •

jeans
cut off T-shirt
cardboard cross sprayed gold
gold chains etc
pair flesh tights
scrap black fur fabric

Knot tights just above crotch to make 'cap' shape to fit over child's hair. Cut off legs and stitch strip of fur down centre from forehead to nape of neck.

• PARTY DRESS •

pink cotton vest
6 m/20 ft long fabric 137 cm/55 in wide

Cut 4 circles as diagram. Cut the radius of each. Sew first 2 circles together at AB, CD to form one skirt, then the second 2 circles in the same way.

If the vest is too long, cut off just below the waist. Cut long strips of lace 4 cm/1½ in wide, gather down centre and sew 2 down front of vest from strap position to bottom edge. Gather the waist of each skirt and sew onto bottom of vest one just above the other. From rest of fabric cut strips of lace about 10 cm/4 in wide, gather up and sew around neck and straps.

Make roses from scraps and sew on.

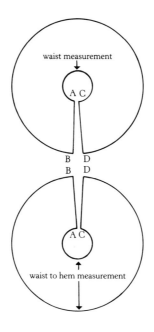

sewing on the neck frill

• PRINCESS •

I made this many years ago from a simple party dress pattern. I adapted it slightly by opening up the front and fitting a gold underskirt behind it. The hat is a simple shape cut from buckram. Decorate dress and hat with remnants of gold fabric, lace and either bought glass jewels or glue and fruit gums as for Queen Elizabeth I.

● SHE-RA ●

30 cm/1 ft brown jersey
scrap brown fur fabric
flesh tights
0.5 m/20 in white jersey or swimsuit
thick piping cord
thin string
Wonderweb
velcro
pasta shapes (domes, leaves, etc)
narrow elastic
white card
gold spray paint
glue
white chocolate buttons

Leotard

Cut as diagram. Sew together side seams and crotch. Elasticate legs and top edge. Make 1.5 cm/½ in straps in same fabric to fasten behind neck with hook and eye. Cut shape in white jersey and Wonderweb for chest area of leotard, as diagram. Iron Wonderweb to back of jersey. Spread glue on each breast piece and coil piping cord, as shown. Spray gold. Cut circles 3.5 cm/

1¼ in diameter in cord, and glue dome pasta or chocolate buttons in centre. Cut leaf shapes and glue string on in vein pattern. Cut tab shapes, glue on pasta or buttons. Spray gold.

Remove paper on Wonderweb from breast piece, and ironing from wrong side of leotard, fix to breast of leotard. Glue on other decorations.

Cuffs

In card, cut 2 shapes as shown. Glue cord around edges, pasta design in centre, and spray gold. Staple on velcro to corners. Sew velcro to straps where they join leotard front.

Head dress

Cut same shape as collar. Glue cord around edge, decorate with dome pasta, and spray gold. Staple elastic to corners, to fit around head.

Boots

Make as for He-Man in brown jersey and fur.

© Mattel Inc. (1988).

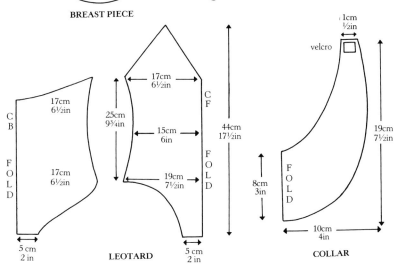

BREAST PIECE

LEOTARD

COLLAR

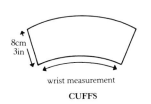

CUFFS

● SKELETON ●

(To fit 4–6 year old)
1 pair black tights (thick)
1 black polo neck jumper
1 skeleton mask, or make your own
white paint, washable
1 black stocking, or half pair of tights

Put the clothes on to the wearer and, if they can bear it, paint in bones as accurately as possible. It feels rather cold and wet but is worth it in the end. Carefully slide off tights and jumper and allow to dry. Wear the stocking over the head with a hole cut for the face and the mask over it.

● SNOWMAN ●

(To fit 6 year old)
2.5 m/100 in medium weight wadding
1.6 m/64 in white wincyette
2 lengths of 10 mm/½ in crin hoop,
1.65 m/41 in and 1.3 m/32 in
1 m/38 in tape
'stones'
scarf, hat and pipe

Cut one piece in wincyette and one piece in wadding as fig. 1.

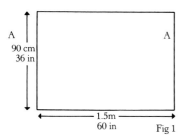

Fig 1

Cut two pieces in wadding only as fig. 2.

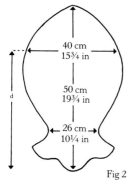

Fig 2

Cut two pieces for balaclava in wadding.

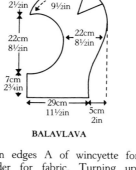

BALAVLAVA

Join edges A of wincyette forming cylinder for fabric. Turning up one 25 mm/1 in at bottom edge B and machine to form channel for bottom hoop. Sew tape to inside half way up to form second channel C. Turn over 25 mm/1 in at top edge D to form third channel for gathering (fig. 3).

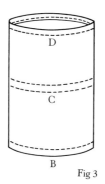

Fig 3

Make slit in top channel and thread tape through ready for gathering. Make two slits 75 mm/3 in apart in each of the other two channels and thread with crin hoop starting with lower channel and longer piece of crin, overlapping 5 cm/2 in and taping together on outside between slits (fig. 4).

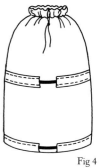

Fig 4

Put shape onto the child, gathering at neck. Wrap wadding around the shape and slipstitch around the bottom edge and at centre front. Tack to neck edge, releasing gathering as necessary. Cut holes for arms. Slipstitch both underarm seams of sleeves marked 'd' on fig. 2, then slipstitch sleeves over armholes taking top of sleeve almost to neck edge. Either leave bottom of sleeve open or slipstitch together, making slit at wrist to allow hands out for eating etc (as in a babygrow). Sew head pieces together.

Tuck headpiece into neck edge. Glue or stitch 'stones' in position. Add hat, scarf and pipe.

● SPIDER-MAN ●

blue leotard
blue tights
1 m/39 in red jersey
Wonderweb
black felt tip pen
narrow elastic
red felt

Make boots and gauntlets as for Superman.

Torso

Cut out shapes in red jersey as diagram, and Wonderweb. Apply Wonderweb to back of shapes, peel off paper, then iron on to front of leotard, back shoulders and upper surface of 2 sleeves.

Hood

Cut 2 shapes, as diagram, sew together along curved edge. Try on and mark eyes and nose. Remove and cut out.

Belt

Cut in red jersey 4 cm/1½ in wide, to child's waist measurement, plus 2.5 cm/1 in overlap for velcro. Back with felt for strength. Now, with felt tip pen, draw web designs on to red parts. Finish with the spider.

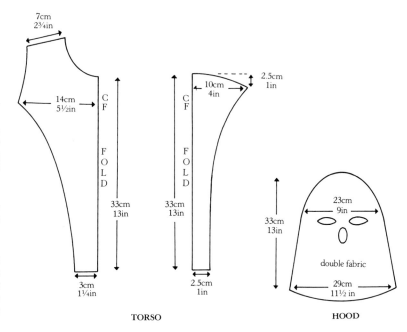

TORSO

HOOD

● SUPERMAN ●

blue leotard
blue tights
1.5 m/5 ft red jersey
red and yellow felt (buy squares
or lengths)
Wonderweb
velcro
narrow elastic

Cloak

Cut as diagram. Make pleat and sew velcro underneath to match velcro on leotard shoulder.

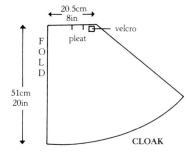

CLOAK

Shorts

Cut as diagram. Sew side seams, hem leg holes, and make channel at waist for elastic, cut to child's waist measurements.

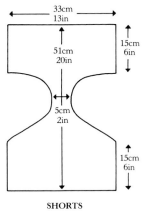

SHORTS

Boots

Cut a pair as diagram. Could use pair of large socks as pattern. Sew front and back seams. Zig-zag narrow elastic around sole. This holds the boot under the soles of the child's shoes. Elasticate tops.

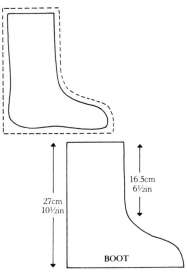

BOOT

Gauntlets

Use a child's glove to draw round. Pin 2 pieces of each glove carefully together and sew round the edge with zig-zag stitch. Turn.

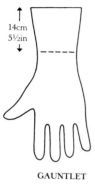

GAUNTLET

Logo

Cut out 2 'S' shapes and 2 backgrounds in Wonderweb. Iron background shapes on to yellow felt, and one 'S' on to yellow, one on to red. Cut out shapes. Peel paper backing from two 'S' shapes and iron one on to each background. Peel paper from backgrounds and iron all yellow logo on to back of cloak, and red/yellow logo on to leotard chest.

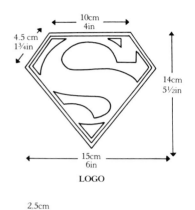

LOGO

Belt

Cut red felt 4 cm/1½ in wide, to fit child's waist. Allow 2.5 cm/1 in overlap and fasten with velcro. Stitch 6 narrow strips of yellow felt along belt, as shown.

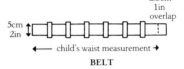

BELT

● WITCH ●

*2 m/78 in black fabric
black card or white card and black
spray paint
coloured wool
tape
glue*

Cloak/dress

Cut as diagram. Sew shoulder–wrist seam and underarm–hem seams. Cut open back neck to allow head through, and zig-zag if fraying. Attach ties to fasten.

Hat

Make cone from card and staple together at base. Cut circular brim as shown. Slash inner edge and bend up tabs. Glue inside rim of cone. Spray black if necessary. Sew lengths of wool onto tape and glue inside rim.

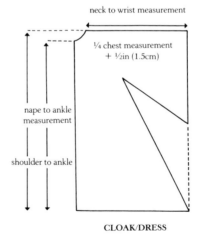

CLOAK/DRESS

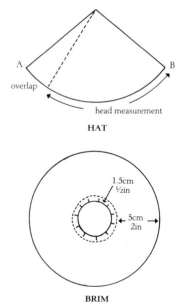

HAT

BRIM

USEFUL ADDRESSES

CATERERS

East Anglia
BIB AND TUCKER
36 Cawston Road
Aylsham
Norwich
Tel: 0263 732872

HAMPERS
69a High Street
Blakeney
Norfolk
Tel: 0263 740801

MARTIN'S CATERING
(party packs)
Evergreen
The Street
Flordon
Norwich
Tel: 0508 470970

Northern England
COOKIE JAR
28 Middleton Park Road
Leeds
Tel: 0532 708504

IMAGINATIVE ICING
(Janice Springall – birthday cakes)
17 Gladstone Road,
Scarborough YO12 7BQ
Tel: 0723 378116

M&B CATERERS
(minimum number 25)
28 Harwell Rise
Churwell
Morley
Leeds LS27 7QN
Tel: 0532 530218

PARTYPLATES
(minimum number 25)
63 Bredbury Green
Romily
Stockport SK6
Tel: 061-430 2608

South-east England
BASKIN ROBINS
(Ice cream cakes)
Tel: 01-575 2004

ANNE FAYRER
(birthday cakes)
66 Lower Sloane Street
London SW1
Tel: 01-730 6277

TESSA CORR
(complete party service)
30 Beckwith Road
London SE24
Tel: 01-274 6196

CRACKERS
(party boxes delivered
throughout Greater London)
Tel: 01-868 4883

FERNS
299 Goring Road
Goring-by-Sea
Worthing
Sussex
Tel: 0903 700442

DUFF & TROTTER
25 Southbank Bus Centre
Ponton Road
London SW8
Tel: 01-627 2770

FIRST PARTIES
(complete party service)
38 Killieser Avenue
London SW2
Tel: 01-671 4196/3507

JILL AND JENNY'S PANTRY
184 Portland Road
Hove
Sussex
Tel: 0273 734261

PARTIPAKS
5 Devon Rise
London N2
Tel: 01-458 7252 or
01-883 8128

PROOKIE'S PUTNEY PARTIES
(complete party service
throughout London)
5 Kelmscot Road
London SW18
Tel: 01-874 3227 or
01-223 1068

South-west England
PENDHU HOUSE
Fore Street
Tintagel
Cornwall
Tel: 0840 770820

Scotland
FOOD FOR THOUGHT
7 Melfont Avenue
Glasgow G41
Tel: 041-427 5554

KAREN CATERING
53 High Street
Paisley PA1
Tel: 041-889 0490 or
041-641 2134

Wales
ANN'S PANTRY
3 Oaklands Park
Port Skewett
Newport
Gwent
Tel: 0291 424228

MRS J's CATERING CO
Lynwood Park View
Pontypool
Tel: 04955 53010

ENTERTAINERS & PARTY EQUIPMENT

East Anglia
M A INFLATABLE HIRE &
ENTERTAINMENTS
(including funfair rides)
24 Fifers Lane
Norwich
Tel: 0603 402834

STEVE SAUSAGE
30 Primrose Close
Mulbarton
Tel: 0508 78837

UNCLE HARRY
273 Southtown Road
Great Yarmouth
Norfolk NR31 0JB
Tel: 0493 655384

Northern England
ARRINGTON'S JUNIOR DISCO
5 Seymour Close
Stretford M16 9DN
Tel: 061-872 7410

DAN DAN THE MAGIC MAN
13 Alresford Road
Middleton M24
Tel: 061-643 5077

WILF DURHAM
(Punch & Judy)
19 Woodbank Drive
Bury
Lancs BL8 1DR
Tel: 061-764 5911

ALLEN JACK
(Musical magician)
189 Whitehall Road
Wyke
Bradford BD12 9LN
Tel: 0274 676218

MR JELLYSPOON & CRISHENDO
(Punch & Judy, clowns & stilt-walkers)
76 Buxton Road
Disley
Stockport SK12 2HE
Tel: 0663 65860

DICK McCULLOGH
(Punch & Judy)
35 Addington Drive
Hadrian Park
Wallsend
Tyne and Wear
Tel: 0632 622438

MYSTER YAFFE
(magician)
422 Street Lane
Leeds LS17 6RL
Tel: 0532 692738

JEFF RICHARDS
(complete party service)
4 Woodbridge Fold
Leeds LS6 3LX
Tel: 0532 759941

South-east England
ALBERT THE IDIOT
c/o Mrs Casey's Music
Glorishears
Thame
Oxford
Tel: 084 421 2231

THE BALLOON WORKS
(party balloons)
233 Sandycombe Road
Kew
Surrey TW9 2EW
Tel: 01-948 8157

CLOPPO & CLOPPETTE
(shows & magic)
Rock Lodge
Washington
W. Sussex RH20 3DA
Tel: 0903 892932

FUNFAIR
(complete party equipment
service)
60 Edgware Way
Middx
Tel: 01-958 6218

BOB GRIGOR
(hire of inflatables and
fun bicycles)
Tel: Slough (0753) 48822

KENSINGTON CARNIVAL
Tel: 01-370 4358

MY BIRTHDAY
Tel: 01-435 6342

OSCAR AND STEPHEN
(magic shows, discos)
9 Hillside Gardens
Edgware
Middx
Tel: 01-958 8158

OSCAR'S DEN
(party shop, including
inflatable hire)
127 Abbey Road
London NW6
Tel: 01-328 6683

PAPERCHASE
(lots of lovely party equipment)
213 Tottenham Court Road
London W1
Tel: 01-580 8496

PARTYMANIA
(complete party equipment
service)
179 Kingston Road
Oxford
Tel: 0865 513397

THE PARTY PLACE
(equipment)
67/69 Gloucester Avenue
London NW1
Tel: 01-586 0169

THE PARTY SHOP
3 Erskine Road
London NW3 3AJ
Tel: 01-722 1478

PATCHY PETE
(clown & magician)
29 Cowper Road
Hemel Hempstead
Herts
Tel: 0442 61767

POM POM PUPPETS &
ENTERTAINMENTS
(including discos)
10 Fulham Park Gardens
London SW6
Tel: 01-736 6532

SMARTIE ARTIE
57 Cutenhoe Road
Luton
Beds
Tel: 0582 459977

JOHN STYLES
(magic shows)
42 Christchurch Road
Sidcup
Kent
Tel: 01-300 3579

THEATRE ZOO
(costumes & party accessories)
21 Earlham Street
London WC2
Tel: 01-836 3150

TRUMPS
(inflatables, roundabouts, entertainers)
Sunny Acres
London Road
Hickstead
W. Sussex RH17 5L2
Tel: 044482 549

'UNCLE' JIM GRAHAM
14 Farm Close
Wallington
Surrey SM6 9PF
Tel: 01-669 1515

REG WEBB
Tel: 01-866 6327

PAUL WINTER
(Punch & Judy, magic)
3 Chalky Road
Portslade
Brighton BN4 2WF
Tel: 0273 420173

South-west England
JOHNNY DOEL
(magic & balloon modelling)
Church Cottage
Church Road
Sparkford
Yeovil
Devon
Tel: 0963 40767

KEN SAVAGE
(comedy magic)
369 Fort Austin Avenue
Crownhill
Plymouth PL6 5TG
Tel: 0752 701090

STAN MARSHALL
(Cornwall's tallest magician)
Red Cove
Mawgan Porth
Newquay
Tel: 0637 860263

Scotland
DOODLES THE CLOWN (Mel Donald)
54 Strathblane Road
Milngavie
Glasgow G62 8DH
Tel: 041-956 4747

MICHAEL BRECK MAGIC SHOWS
78 Nevis Road
Bearsden
Glasgow G61 4LF
Tel: 041-942 1114

KIDDIES RIDES
10 Jordanvale Avenue
Glasgow G14
Tel: 041-954 8959

SCOTT LOVAT
(Punch & Judy)
65 Scotstoun Park
S. Queensferry
Edinburgh EH30
Tel: 031-331 1986

Wales
ACE CHILDREN'S ENTERTAINMENTS
(complete party service & shows)
Ton Cottage
Tredunnock
Usk
Newport
Tel: 0783 4975 or
          063349 607

HIGH ENERGY INFLATABLES
(indoor & outdoor)
Bwlch-Gwyn Farm
Ystradowen
S. Glamorgan
Tel: 044 63 3342

PADDY THE CLOWN
5 Connaught Road
Roath
Cardiff
Tel: 0222 798860

PROFESSOR MYSTRAL'S JUVENILE
OMNIBUS
65 Penylan Road
Cardiff
Tel: 0222 485544

THE PLAY MACHINE
(children's theatre company)
12 Manor Road
Canton
Cardiff CP5 1PF
Tel: 0222 222270

PARTY PLACES

McDONALD'S HAMBURGERS LTD
(Head office)
11 High Road
London N2
Tel: 01-883 6400

PIZZAEXPRESS LTD
(Head office)
29 Wardour Street
London W1
Tel: 01-437 7215

Little Chef, Burger King, Wimpy and many
smaller fast food places also offer party
facilities. Telephone your nearest branch for
details.

SKATING RINKS, SWIMMING POOLS,
SPORTS/LEISURE CENTRES
These places are often owned/operated by local
authorities. Check in Yellow Pages, or ask your
local town hall for details.

UNUSUAL PLACES

HMS BELFAST
Symons Wharf
Vine Lane
London SE1
Tel: 01-407 6434

CUTTY SARK
King William Walk
London SE10
Tel: 01-858 3445

NATURAL HISTORY MUSEUM
(has a private room – does not allow children's
parties among exhibits)
Cromwell Road
London SW7
Tel: 01-589 8934

Your local museums and places of historical
interest may well have special party facilities;
phone them and ask. To make the hire more
economical, you could share the cost with the
families of children who have birthdays around
the same time.

OTHER PARTY IDEAS

It isn't necessary to have large numbers to
make a party successful. An outing to the zoo,
cinema, theatre or theme park makes a lovely
treat and could be restricted to the birthday
child and two or three special friends.